fash  nake

ses

Fun and colourful mini-rucksack (see Chapter 7).

design & make
fashion bags
and purses

CHRISTINA BRODIE

A & C Black

For fashionistas everywhere

First published in Great Britain 2009
A&C Black Publishers
36 Soho Square
London W1D 3QY
www.acblack.com

ISBN 978-0-7136-8869-6

Book design: Penny Mills and Sutchinda Thompson
Cover design: Sutchinda Thompson
Commissioning Editor: Susan James
Managing Editor: Sophie Page
Copyeditor: Carol Waters

Printed and bound in China

contents

1 introduction

This book intends to provide a fun introduction to making fashion bags and purses for a number of different occasions – whether for everyday, holiday or evening wear. Using simple interpretations of fashionable shapes, it covers fabric selection; decoration with various notions, beads and trims; making up using both hand and machine construction; and a practical chapter on how to design your own bag through simple pattern cutting.

Most of the bags should be able to be made in a weekend, or even several hours. Many are relatively easy and uncomplicated to make; I've tried to make the construction as logical and straightforward as I possibly can. If you choose to make several models from this book you will become aware of different methods of construction or fabric manipulation and ways in which they can be used. The original designs are copyright, so are for home use only; however, they can be altered in a number of ways to create new and original designs.

Patterns for each bag are provided towards the end of the book. Those drawn on a grid should be scaled up; the sides of each large square within the grid correspond to 5 cm (2 in.). Elsewhere, dimensions have been given, notably where patterns are either particularly simple or complex.

I use leather for one of the purses in this book, and for some buckle details; however, this book is generally concerned with designing with 'fabrics' in the wider sense, and most of the bags in this book fall into the 'soft fabric bags' category. The fabrics and designs used have been intended to be friendly to your domestic machine and easy to work with. The bags also aim to be as practical as possible, or at least to fulfil the purpose for which they were originally conceived. I have tried to include as much variety in shape as I can, and I hope the selection of ideas on offer will inspire you and motivate you to create fashion bags of your own!

I would like to thank Susan James, of A & C Black, and all others who have offered me continued encouragement and support; thanks is also due to the suppliers of the various materials used in this book, for their invaluable contribution.

Christina Brodie
May 2008

opposite: Coin purse wth rhinestone decoration (see Chapter 5).

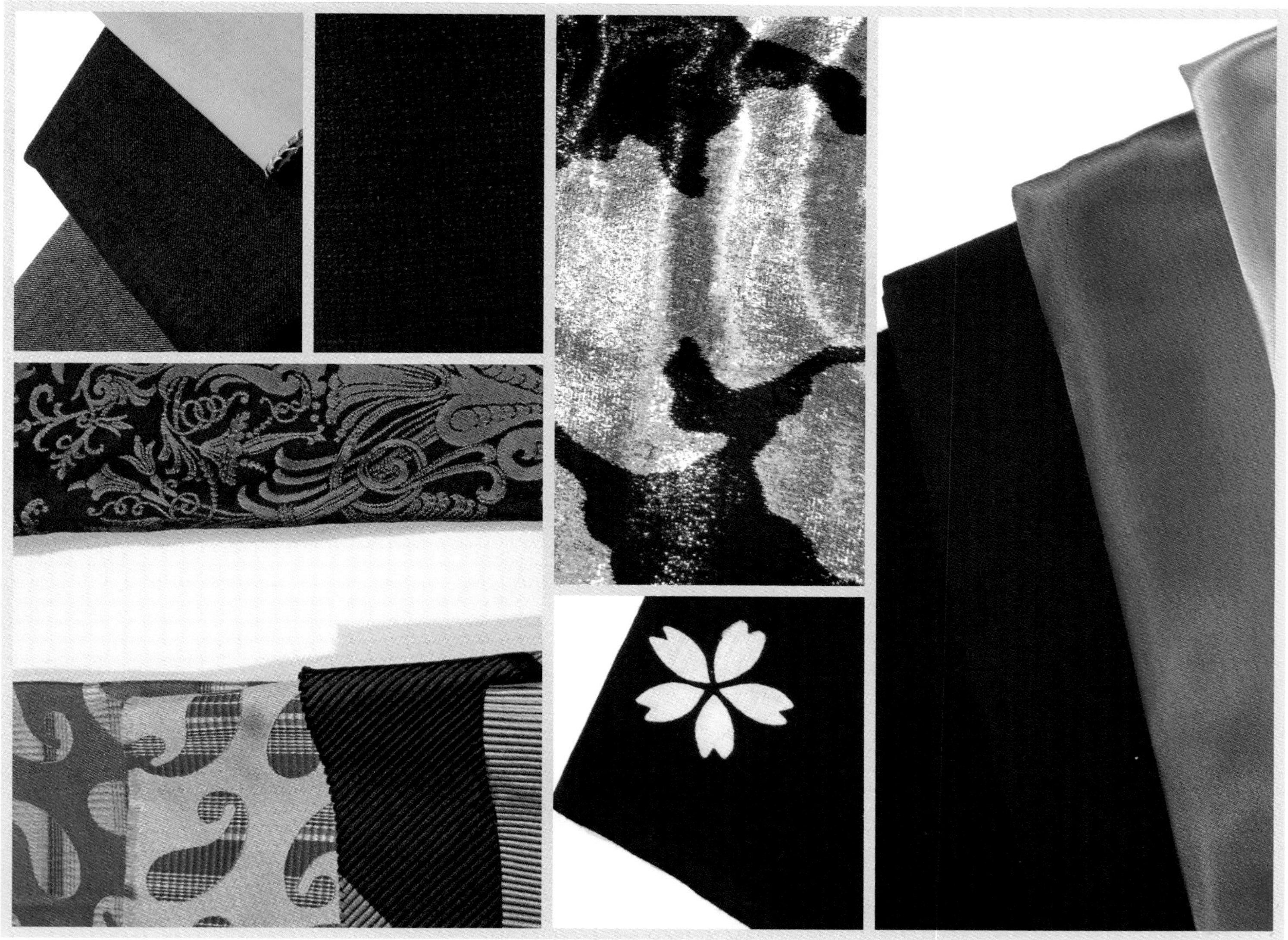

2 materials and techniques

Across the following pages you will find illustrated some of the materials that are used in this book. However, these are not proscriptive but specifically relate to the materials that were chosen for each pattern and that were felt to be particularly suitable.

Within the materials recommendations for each chapter you will find that I don't specify quantities of fabric. This is because you may choose to use alternative fabrics with different widths. What is important here is whether the pattern fits the fabric and whether the fabric's grain orientation is correct over all the pattern pieces. Draw the pattern pieces out beforehand, either by scaling up or tracing the designs found at the back of the book. Mark them up with all relevant information (see Chapter 13), and take them with you whilst fabric-hunting.

A note on buying quantities of fabric and materials: fabric suppliers normally sell fabric in minimum quantities, especially if the fabric is an unusual one; therefore, considerable amounts of fabric may be left at the end of a project. It can, however, be prudent to overbuy on occasion (as, for example, fabric pieces may need to be re-cut if mistakes have been made). Try to identify several projects that you would like to make from the book, or design your own, and use up the excess materials in this way.

If you want to use lighter-weight fabrics for bags, it is recommended you use a fusible fabric or other stiffening or support fabric. This is to strengthen your bag and preserve its shape so it won't immediately collapse once it has been loaded up. I recommend a firm but lightweight fusible such as Vilene® H250 for lightweight fabrics and a heavier fusible drill for medium weight fabrics. Canvas and denims need much less support, and the designs using canvas and denim in this book actually use no support at all.

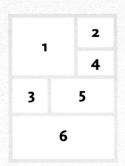

1 Tie silks and silk brocade.
2 Assortment of denims.
3 Japanese print cotton.
4 Canvas fabric.
5 Lamé fabric.
6 Mesh fabric (used as a lining), poplin, acetate lining fabrics.

If you haven't used many of the materials in this book before, you should find most of them surprisingly easy to work with. They can be broadly broken down into several categories:

FABRICS (WOVENS)

Tie silk – this is available in many different colours and weights. It may be either single-sided or double-sided and is not usually of a very generous width. That having been said, the best tie silks are spectacular; some are double-sided with a different pattern on both sides, opening up a wide range of possibilities. They are easy to sew, generally fairly stable fabrics, and the reflective quality of the silk emphasizes their jewel-like colours. I recommend using silk thread for tacking, since this does not leave holes in the fabric when removed.

Cottons, including denims – Printed Indian or ethnic cottons, such as the Japanese printed cotton used for the Exotic Fabrics Bag in Chapter 6, are my favourites from this group of fabrics, due to their softness, their vibrancy and their simplicity yet richness of pattern. Depending on the finish, cottons can have a shiny or matt appearance and be very crisp or very soft. I prefer a 'natural' look and feel, tending to gravitate towards the 'ethnic' types of cottons more than those of Western design. A softer handle and appearance is more pleasing to sight and touch, and does not show up marks as much. Denim is made using a twill weave, and as such is very compact and hardwearing, although if threads are pulled it can fray easily. It is unlikely to need additional stiffening or support from a fusible as it keeps a certain amount of shape well.

Canvas – this is an excellent choice for bags as it is tough and hardwearing; as with denim, there is no particular need to line it (it can be neatened with zigzag). It is also very easy to sew. Although it may seem plain and dull when bought, it can easily be smartened up through choice of notions and decoration. See Chapters 3 and 12 for two different bag styles using the exact same dark brown canvas fabric; the matt dark brown of the canvas in each case contrasts with both harmonizing and colourful shiny or semi-shiny decorative materials.

Miscellaneous synthetic fabrics – any fabric with sufficient strength and stability can be made effectively into a bag. Lining will also contribute towards giving the bag extra body; for example, the Exotic Fabrics Bag in Chapter 6 uses a combination of the Japanese cotton print fabric (above) that is quilted to give the bag upper stability, and a bold black-and-gold lamé synthetic fabric that is lined with a red and green shot acetate lining. This is an example of how supposedly disparate fabrics can combine with great success.

Lining fabrics – a number of fabrics can be used as a lining, whether it is self-fabric or a proprietary lining fabric, depending on the desired effect. I like a shot acetate lining, but this can have a tendency to snag or be marked easily. For a more hardwearing finish I would choose a dark-coloured cotton poplin; it has a matt surface, so does not show up marks easily, and is also easier to clean and sew. For a more 'sporty' or up-to-date feel, I have used a polyester/nylon mesh fabric with minimal stretch along its width for the City Bag lining in Chapter 11. Experiment and see what works!

FABRICS (KNITS)

Fake fur – this is usually mounted onto either a compact knit or woven backing; if knit, there may be an element of stretch to the fabric. It is a preferable alternative to (and nowadays virtually indistinguishable from), the real thing. The one drawback is that it can be rather messy to cut due to fibre shedding. The bag in Chapter 8 uses a lightweight fur fabric with low pile, mounted on a fusible drill. You may hear me refer to this fabric alternatively as faux fur.

FABRICS (NONWOVENS)

Leather – the ease of cutting, punching and general stability of leather make it a good choice for finishing a number of accessories with buckles. For buckles, I have used a relatively thick cowhide leather – 0.15 cm ($^1/_{16}$ in.) thickness, which can be marked reasonably easily with fineliners or a pencil and cut with sharp fabric scissors. This isn't a book about leathercraft, and the constraints of the project don't demand that a simple buckle will need to be finished in any particular way; all that matters is that the cutting of the pieces is neat and straight.

However, you may also want to use a different weight of leather for appliqué or to make small leather items such as purses. Good leather can be quite expensive when bought as a skin, and because of the differential stretch over parts of the skin, variable in quality; a good part of the skin may go to waste. It can be more economical to buy old leather garments from discount leather stores and cut them up; that way the quality of the leather is more uniform and predictable. With prudent cutting you can also use the lining of the garment to make pockets or bag/purse linings – a great way to recycle and create one-off pieces in the process!

Plastics – pure plastic fabric (as opposed to PVC fabric, which is made of a PVC coating on a fabric base) is used as a functional lining in this book. It is glued to hold it firm (Copydex® glue is effective for a temporary bond of this type, and should be left to dry thoroughly overnight) and then stitched into position. There are a large variety of plastic fabrics on the market; for this book I use a translucent plastic with a slightly rubbery feel as lining for waterproof pockets.

Thin fake fur fabric.

Plastic for lining.

FABRICS (FUSIBLES/STIFFENERS)

Vilene® – this is available in a number of different weights and thicknesses. It is generally reckoned that a fusible material should be lighter in weight than the cloth it supports, though this need not always be the case. Generally, lighter-weight fabrics should partner with a lightweight but firm fusible material; heavier-weight fabrics with a heavier fusible.

I have a personal preference for Vilene® H250, (lightweight but firm) and Vilene® H640 (wadding material, suitable for quilting and very good in tandem with soft cottons). The ironing times and settings are printed on the side of the fabric.

Fusible drill – this is a strong and tough fusible, great for stiffening heavier fabrics or for larger bags which are subjected to a greater load and need to be stabilized to prevent tearing, stretching or loss of shape of the outer fabric. It is also very good for backing fabrics with a slight stretch, such as leatherette.

Buckram – this is popularly used for millinery; it is reasonably coarse, formed of an open weave and stiff due to its impregnation with glue. The term 'buckram' is a generic one and can be applied to a variety of stiffening fabrics; the type of 'buckram' used for lining collars has a finer weave and is not impregnated with glue. It can be used for bag bottoms or areas which need a more rigid structure. I actually try to avoid rigidity and a distinct 'bottom' to bags (as they tend to be uncomfortable to sew on a home sewing machine) preferring instead to form the bag bottom through darting or tucks, for example, and to use a heavier shell fabric together with a fusible drill.

Buckram, fusible drill, Vilene® iron-on fusibles.

tools

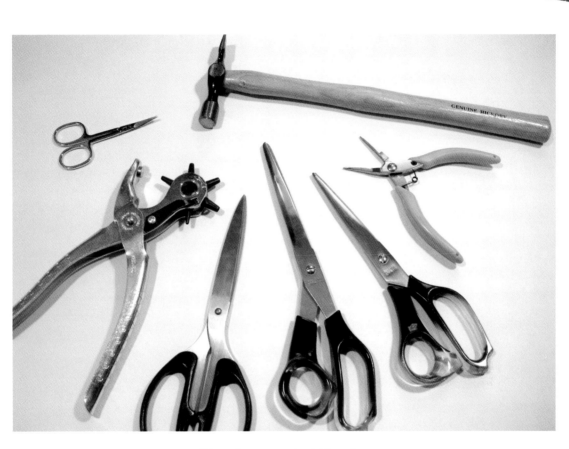

Scissors, hammer, punch, miniature pliers.

Fabric scissors – these should be used for cutting fabrics only, never paper, as this can blunt the blades. Good fabric scissors should be able to cut a wide range of materials, including leather of a medium thickness. Check the sharpness of your scissors on a regular basis.

Paper scissors – these will be invaluable for pattern-making. I recommend good all-purpose scissors as opposed to tiny paper scissors, since they save time when cutting out and are easier on the hands.

Hammer – an ordinary hammer will be useful for fixing hardware such as eyelets and snap fasteners.

Revolving fabric punch – capable of making holes of various sizes, I use this mainly for punching holes in leather (although a standard punch which comes as part of an eyelet set can be used just as effectively).

Miniature pliers – these are particularly useful when fixing the prongs of magnetic clasps.

PINS AND NEEDLES

T-shaped pins – it is well worth investing in a box of T-shaped pins as opposed to dressmaking pins. These are useful for a number of projects, including millinery projects, and do not easily 'disappear' into the item. A large box is expensive but well worth the investment. They are thicker than ordinary pins, but I do not find that this affects the result.

General sewing needles – I use quilting needles as these are short and slender and thus easier to do fine work with. I recommend a standard packet of size 5/10 needles, which will stand you in good stead for a number of projects. Or, a needle set incorporating a number of needles of about 3.8 cm (1½ in.), with a square head and small-to-medium-sized eye, will be ideal. This type of needle is very easy to manipulate and handle.

Beading needles – these will be necessary for items involving bead embroidery, since the head of most conventional sewing needles is far too thick to go through the middle of most beads.

THREAD

Silk threads – these are suitable for projects involving silk fabrics, since cotton or cotton poly-ester will 'pull' the fabric too much. Where an item is made with a silk fabric I also try to tack it with a silk thread. This may at first glance seem a waste, but cotton is a much thicker and harsher fibre and can leave marks in the silk when the tacking threads are removed. Thus, silk thread is also useful for tacking satin-weave lining fabrics (whatever the fibre content).

Polyester sewing threads – these are available in a wide range of colours and are highly suitable for most projects. Topstitching thread is a thicker vari-ant of ordinary sewing thread and should be used for decorative topstitching only; when topstitch-ing, the bobbin should be threaded with ordinary sewing thread.

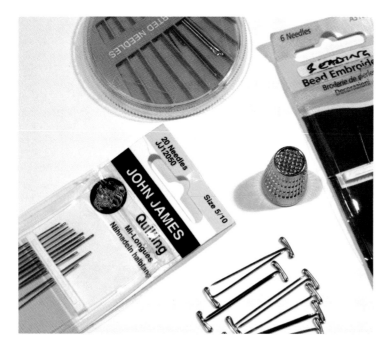

left: Pins and needles.
above: Polycotton, silk and topstitching threads.

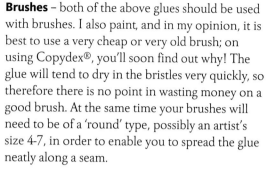

GLUES, BRUSHES AND ADHESIVE TAPES

PVA glue – this is a light craft glue suitable for pre-sticking soft dress leathers (see Chapter 12) prior to sewing. I don't recommend it for bonding the seams of fabrics such as leatherette or plastic fabrics since it is too light and doesn't have enough grip.

Copydex® – this is a very good all-purpose adhesive. It smells and looks strange on application, but dries clear. Excess dried glue can also be rolled off the surface gently. This type of glue is suitable for sticking leathers and plastic (see Chapter 4).

Brushes – both of the above glues should be used with brushes. I also paint, and in my opinion, it is best to use a very cheap or very old brush; on using Copydex®, you'll soon find out why! The glue will tend to dry in the bristles very quickly, so therefore there is no point in wasting money on a good brush. At the same time your brushes will need to be of a 'round' type, possibly an artist's size 4-7, in order to enable you to spread the glue neatly along a seam.

Nail glue or superglue – this is good for bonding items such as rhinestones to surfaces such as leather. I don't personally find hot-fix applicators, that are available to fix rhinestones, very effective as the glue is not strong enough. Superglue generally only really works well on surfaces that aren't fibrous, and is not generally suitable for non-leather fabrics.

❝ NB Care must be taken when handling superglue, as skin and eyes can be easily bonded within seconds. If it does splash on skin, follow the manufacturer's advice for removal, or sand the area gently when dry with fine sandpaper. Do not attempt to peel glue away from skin, as the glue layer will invariably take several layers of skin with it. ❞

It is not recommended that glues should be used exclusively as a substitute for stitching, as this will not bond seams sufficiently. A good general practice, especially when sewing leather, is to stick seams together before stitching an item if the seams cannot be tacked.

Adhesive tapes – these are useful for attaching pattern pieces to one another in the design stage to check the fit, or for making a larger sheet of paper out of two smaller pieces. Easiest to work with, because of its matt top surface, is invisible tape; Sellotape® gives the best adhesion.

PVA, Copydex® and nail glues.

PAPER AND DRAWING EQUIPMENT, FABRIC MARKERS

Layout paper – this is great for planning and sketching designs and making patterns since it is semi-transparent. Buy a large (A3) size since this offers more flexibility when designing larger items. If for any reason you run out of paper when making a pattern, or the item's dimensions are greater than the paper, tape two sheets of paper together using Sellotape®.

Tracing paper – this can be used for making mirrored designs, although layout paper, because of its transparency, can be just as effective. An A4 size block is usually adequate.

Thin art card – for making master patterns (that paper patterns can be made from).

Propelling pencil – use for sketching designs and pattern drafting.

Ordinary drawing pencil – one with a soft lead is good for tracing patterns and marking leather.

Biro – this is actually very good for transferring patterns from chalked paper onto leather due to the pressure exerted by the pen tip.

Fineliner pens – I buy packets of these in 0.1, 0.3, 0.5 and 0.7 mm sizes. They are good for making final patterns and also for marking leather.

Fineliner pens, propelling pencil, layout paper.

Draughtsman's eraser – for erasing when pattern drafting. I tend to prefer a draughtsman's eraser over a putty rubber, as putty rubbers leave a thin film of oil on the drawing surface, which attracts dirt.

Rulers and set squares – large rulers (approx. 45 cm (18 in.) length) and set squares are invaluable for pattern-making.

Protractors, compasses and French curves – protractors will help you measure angles accurately; compasses and French curves will enable you to create good, smooth curves within a pattern.

The following are also very effective for marking fabric:

Tailor's chalk – available in several different colours, but mainly white; good for transferring designs.

White pencil – this is good for marking dark-coloured fabrics. It does not need to be a specific fabric marker, but can be an ordinary artist's white pencil; it should be reasonably soft to allow the design to be transferred easily.

I don't always mark fabric; often I pin the pattern to the fabric and cut round it. However, fabric markers of any type can be useful, for example, when making carrying straps without a pattern.

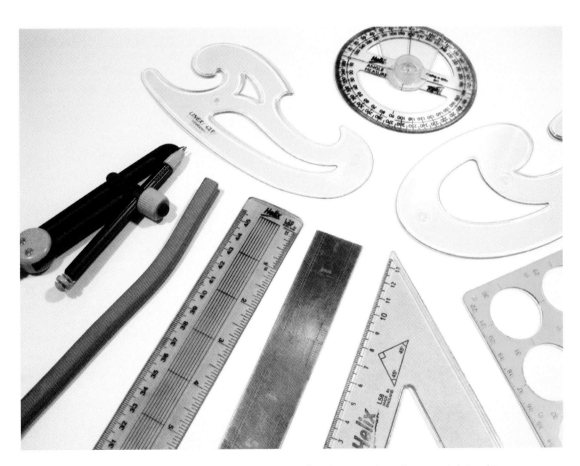

Compasses, protractors, French curves, rulers, set squares, circle template.

NOTIONS, FASTENINGS AND MISCELLANEOUS ITEMS

These include feathers (trim bought by the metre), tassels (bought as a trim or singly, usually for furnishing use), beads, rhinestones and found materials, toggles and fastenings. Depending on the type of product, both retailers and wholesalers will sell a minimum quantity of these items, or sell them packeted, rather than individually, since the unit price decreases when the item is bought in bulk. When buying materials of this type, it is a good idea to have a number of projects in mind that they could be used for.

Feathers – trims are bought by the metre, with the feathers sewn into a band, and should be considered a luxury, as they are often very expensive. The least expensive tend to be undyed iridescent cock feathers. When using a sew-on feather trim, the trim edge will need to be concealed in some way, either through hiding in a seam or covering with an additional trim.

Vintage trims – an air of authenticity is brought to a fashion piece through vintage trims, wherever their origin: for example, the vintage Indian shisha mirror trim in Chapter 10.

Ribbons and braids – there are a wide variety of decorative ribbons on the market. Satin ribbons are available either double-faced or as a binding, in which case the edges are folded over towards the back. Most are synthetic, but the ribbon used in this book is bias-cut silk diagonally joined at intervals. Leather and suede trims are also joined diagonally in this way and, because of the consistency necessary to make a good quality leather trim, are very expensive.

Depending on the context, furnishing braids may also not be out of place. A thin furnishing braid is used for the Indian Bag in Chapter 10; the colours, textures and weight harmonize well with the item.

Cords – these may be used, twisted around each other, to create an alternative carrying strap or handle. This is another instance where a furnishing notion, carefully chosen, can work in a 'bag' context – see the Butterfly Bag in Chapter 12.

Polypropylene – this is used in much commercial bag manufacturing and is available in a variety of widths and colours. It is used for carrying straps. Although tough, and difficult to cut, it is surprisingly easy to sew.

Piping cord – this is often used in combination with a self or other binding to provide a decorative finish to bag edges. I actually use several lengths sandwiched between denim fabric in Chapter 11 to make a reinforced carrying strap.

Tassels – these are good for creating an 'ethnic' look. Use dress,

Feather trim.

top: Polypropylene for bag straps, bindings, piping cord, decorative furnishing cord.
above: Beads and sequins.

trim, as feathers, singly, or in colour-coordinated packets. When applied singly (as opposed to a sew-on trim), a beading needle should be used as this has a thin head which will pass much more easily through the centre of small seed beads.

Sequins – these may be of many types; large sequins with a hold at one edge are good for producing the effect of 'fish scales' when overlapped. Smaller sequins may be stitched singly (with a bead holding them into position), or in chains, to produce a decorative effect.

Rhinestones – these may be sew-on, hot-fix stones (applied using a heated applicator), or simply need to be glued. I prefer not to 'hot-fix' myself, being more in favour of superglue. Swarovski® rhinestones come in a variety of colours, styles and shapes including round, teardrop, leaf and square shapes. Patterns that successfully combine all these elements are well worth the effort to create (see Chapter 5).

Bells – these may be used in clusters to, again, create a fun ethnic look. Don't overuse them, as this will be obvious and excessive (see Chapter 10).

Decorative buttons – these can be used not only as decoration but to disguise carrying strap or handle attachment points (see Chapter 11).

and not furnishing, tassels; the latter are very obviously 'furnishing' and may well look slightly odd when used in a dress context.

Elastic – this is useful for areas of the design which allow for 'give', such as the edge of a lined pocket (see Chapter 11). Elastic doesn't tend to be used much in bag design, since an element of rigidity in a bag is generally preferred.

Beads – these can be bought as a

Eyelets and snap fasteners – these are supplied in packs and should come with their own tools and instructions enclosed; these will vary according to the manufacturer. It is a good idea, if unfamiliar with the technique, to buy more of this type of product than you need, and especially to check whether it is compatible with your chosen material and pattern.

Buckles, D-rings and metal hoops – a generic selection is generally available, mainly in metal or plastic. It is essential that a buckle strap is compatible with the buckle itself. This means that the strap should be neither too narrow nor too wide, but be able to be comfortably done, undone and pulled through. The design should take account of this. D-rings and metal hoops are used to fasten and strengthen carrying straps, (see Chapter 6 or Chapter 7).

Zips – these are a popular, successful and secure method of bag closure. Match the size and weight of the zip to the size and weight of the bag; for example, a lighter weight dress zip will be more suitable for lighter weight materials. A zip that is too heavy will always look too stiff, although this effect could, if desired, be used for design purposes.

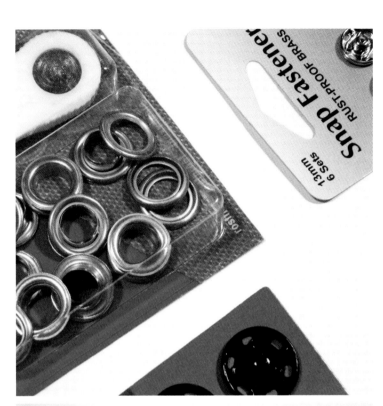

top: Eyelets and snap fasteners.
above: Dress weight zip.

Purse frames – these consist of a frame into which the purse body is glued, with a clip for closing the purse. When constructing a purse of this type the pattern should be carefully measured and perhaps even made up in calico beforehand to check that the fit is absolutely correct.

SEWING MACHINE

Any machine will be suitable for the projects in this book, assuming they are at least able to stitch through several layers of denim fabric, and 2 layers of 0.15 cm ($^1/_{16}$ in.) thickness cowhide leather.

Straight and zigzag stitches are necessary, as is a plentiful supply of sewing-machine needles for ordinary, leather and fine fabrics. You will also need a zipper foot. I find this incredibly useful for all kinds of things, not just to insert zips, but to edge buckles or topstitch the edges of bags made from bulky fabrics, stitch fastenings or handles into position, apply bindings or appliqué, or use piping cord.

A roller foot may be suitable for some fabrics, such as plastics or certain ribbons, that are difficult to push through the machine using an ordinary foot. I also use a quilting attachment to create the equidistantly spaced quilting in Chapter 6. This can be set to a particular width and used to space the sewing lines. As part of my sewing-machine equipment, it screws into the zipper foot; check your machine specifications to see whether such an item is available for your machine. If not, I give instructions for making the item in an alternative way.

SEWING TECHNIQUES

Machine patchwork, machine embroidery (using topstitching thread) and machine appliqué are all used in this book, together with some handsewing and embroidery. Handsewing or machine-sewing can be substituted for each other when practicalities make it difficult to sew in one or the other way.

The various sewing techniques used are covered in the relevant chapters; for example, a method of sewing sequins is shown in Chapter 12. For much handsewing, which is mainly used for sewing up linings, attaching braids, and so forth, I use a variant of hemstitching or oversewing, using small, imperceptible stitches. To catch fabric in an area, I make what I call a few 'catch' stitches (several small stitches in one spot) to secure the fabric at that point.

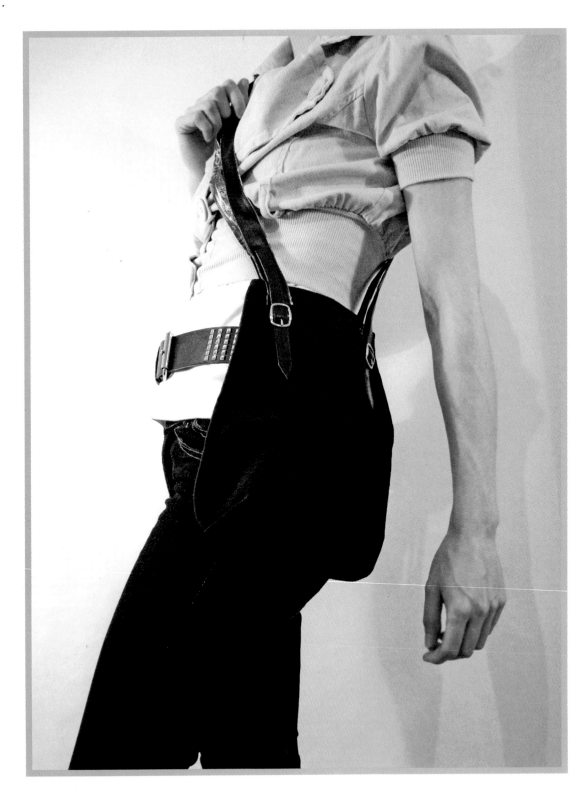

3 canvas bag

This bag is made from practical medium-weight canvas and given extra shape through darting at the base. The carrying straps attached at either side are long enough for the bag to be worn across the body. They are made from lengths of two types of ribbon binding machined together: one a colourful silk ribbon, the other a dark navy synthetic ribbon binding. The silk ribbon is slightly wider than the synthetic ribbon, which creates a flash of colour when the bag is worn. The ribbon carrying straps are themselves reinforced by straps cut from brown leather, and gold effect buckles. Finally, the bag is closed with an oversized snap fastener sewn just inside the top edge.

Canvas is strong and very easy to sew, needing only a zigzag stitch around the edges to neaten it sufficiently. This bag is not lined and does not have pockets; most of the stitching is machine-stitching. To give you an idea of the size of the bag, it is large enough to carry a very slim A5 notebook and writing materials.

step-by-step method

Some of the materials you will need: silk satin ribbon binding, Copydex®, synthetic ribbon binding, revolving punch, leather, canvas, buckles.

YOU WILL NEED

- Canvas
- Cowhide leather pieces (for buckles), 0.15 cm (¹⁄₁₆ in.) thick
- Synthetic satin ribbon binding, 2 cm (³⁄₄ in.)wide, 230 cm (2¹⁄₂ yds) long

- Silk satin ribbon binding, 2.5 cm (1 in.) wide, 230 cm (2¹⁄₂ yds) long
- Matching polyester thread
- Needle
- Pins
- Fabric scissors

- White pencil
- Revolving punch
- 4 x 1.5 cm (⁵⁄₈ in.) buckles
- 1 large 1.9 cm (³⁄₄ in.)snap fastener
- Sewing machine with zipper foot

For pattern see page 139.

Mark the outline of the pattern and position of the darts on the WS (wrong side) of the canvas using a white pencil.

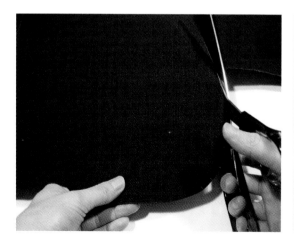

Cut out the canvas pattern pieces.

Fold the fabric and stitch the dart from the edge of the bag to its point as marked.

Pin the two halves of the bag together RS (right side) to RS and stitch.

Fold under the top edge 1.3 cm ($^1/_2$ in.), pin and stitch.

Topstitch all the sides of the bag up to where the bag begins to curve, stopping short at the point where a line projected from the end of the dart would form a right-angle with the bag side.

To make the carrying strap, place the ribbon bindings together WS to WS and stitch them along both sides, so that the coloured binding provides a flash of colour along the inside edge of the plainer binding.

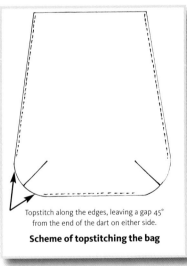

Topstitch along the edges, leaving a gap 45° from the end of the dart on either side.

Scheme of topstitching the bag

Mark the positions for the buckles with a cross and white pencil 2.5 cm (1 in.) from the top edge and 3.8 cm (1 ¹/₂ in.) from each side.

Carefully trace around the buckle strap pattern onto the leather pieces with a fineliner pen; make four buckle straps.

Cut out the buckle straps and punch them using a revolving fabric punch.

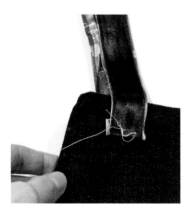

Tack the ends of the ribbon to the points marked with a cross, turning their ends under.

Stitch the ends of the ribbon using a zipper foot.

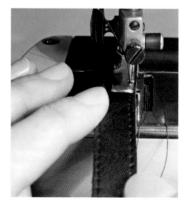

Topstitch the leather buckle straps close to their edges using the zipper foot.

Handstitch the buckles by their central posts directly below the ends of the ribbon.

Thread the buckle straps through the buckles so that the distance to which they extend up the ribbon is equal for all attachment points.

Apply a thin film of Copydex® glue to the very ends of the leather buckle straps to bond the buckle straps and ribbon lightly prior to sewing. The glue should not be so thick that it penetrates through to the silk ribbon on the other side.

Sew the top of the buckle strap to the ribbon using the zipper foot.

The finished bag.

4 yummy mummy bag

This bag is classic, stylish and no-nonsense, and designed for stashing 'baby' kit in; it's extremely practical, with discreet plastic-lined pockets on either side, and a generous interior which boasts additional pockets, including one for a mobile phone – or baby bottle, whichever you prefer! Made in a classic Op Art-patterned fabric, it's not obviously 'baby' and thus very suitable for working mums, since it teams well with a business suit. Artists will also love this bag; the plastic-lined pockets are ideal for temporary transport of damp brushes or sponges, and made with brightly coloured contrast zips.

The bag is fastened with a magnetic clasp and lined with self-fabric; no extra stiffening materials are needed, as the material is medium-weight and has reasonable bulk. For practical purposes, I would personally recommend avoiding any overtly light-coloured fabrics, choosing instead darker fabrics with a dense pattern.

I would recommend taking a weekend or so to make the bag, since the plastic parts need to be glued and it may take a while for the glue to dry since the plastic is a non-porous surface; it's best to go off and do something else in the interim!

step-by-step method

Some of the materials you will need: Op Art fabric, plastic, Copydex® glue, tacking and sewing threads, magnetic clasp, needle, tailor's chalk or white pencil, fineliner, brush, zips.

YOU WILL NEED

▶ Medium-weight linen-style Op Art or similar fabric

▶ Plastic (for pocket linings)

▶ Matching sewing thread

▶ Tacking thread

▶ Needle

▶ Tailor's chalk (or white pencil)

▶ Fineliner (for marking plastic)

▶ Old brush

▶ Copydex® glue

▶ Fabric scissors

▶ 2 contrast zips, approx. 30cms (12in.)

▶ Sewing machine with zipper foot

For pattern see pages 140-142.

This bag is self-lined. Cut out all pieces in the outer/lining fabric. If the pattern has a direction, the direction of the pattern on the pattern pieces should face the same way on one side of the bag, whether it be outside or inside. It doesn't matter if the pattern directions aren't the same for the outside and inside, so long as the warp or weft run parallel to the bottom edge of the bag; all that matters is that the outsides or the insides form a coherent unit, with the pattern running the same way along their length or width.

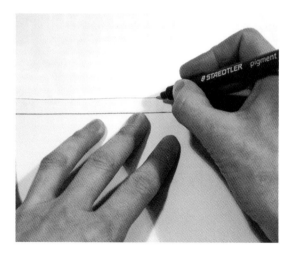

Place the plastic lining pattern pieces onto the plastic; direction of placement is not so important here as plastic is of a uniform nature and non-directional. Draw round the plastic lining pattern pieces, marking the plastic with a fineliner pen.

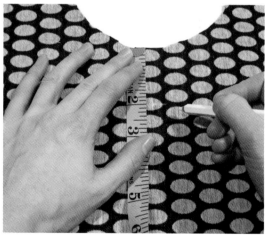

Measure 5 cm (2 in.) down from the centre of the top curve of the self-fabric lining and mark the point with a cross using tailor's chalk or white pencil. Do this for both sides of the self-fabric lining. On one side of the lining, also mark the positions for the combination pocket.

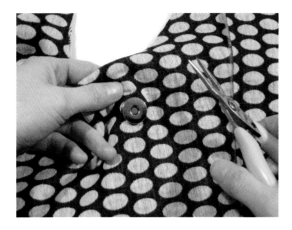

Insert one half of the magnetic clasp into either side of the self-fabric lining. You may need to use a set of pliers to ensure that the pins of the clasp are securely fixed.

Cut strips of spare fabric 2.5 cm (1 in.) by 15 cm (6 in.) and fold them over each end of the zip, tacking them into position. Where there is excess length present in the zip, use one of the outer fabric notched pattern pieces to measure the zip and then tack over the teeth with a few stitches, so that when the excess is cut away the fly will not come off the end.

Stitch the pieces of fabric to the ends of the zip using a zipper foot.

Tack and stitch a 0.6 cm (¹/₄ in.) hem around the combination pocket piece.

Tack and stitch a 0.6 cm (¹/₄ in.) hem along both sides of the carrying handle.

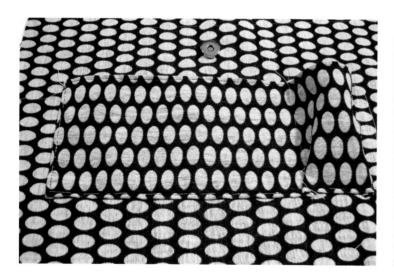

Tack the pocket piece to the lining as shown, using the notches in the pattern to help you. The mobile phone compartment is created by folding the excess fabric towards the pattern points on either side, making tucks. This will ensure that the mobile phone does not 'pop out' of its pocket.

Stitch the combination pocket to the bag lining using a zipper foot, to enable you to stitch close to the edge.

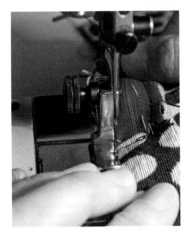

Tack and then stitch the zip on to the top and bottom self-fabric sections that make up the lower half of the front of the bag, using a zipper foot.

Join the sections making up the lower half of the bag. Tack and stitch either end of the sections together that are not covered by the zip.

Topstitch closely over the edges of the fabric adjacent to the zip, working from one end to the other so that the seams are fully flattened down.

Using Copydex®, glue the top piece of the plastic pocket into position. Glue it so that its lower edge aligns with the lower edge of the zip. This will make sewing much easier. Wait until the glue is completely dry (transparent). Then re-stitch over the top-stitching lines on the RS in order to secure the plastic in position.

Trim the excess plastic off at its lower edge closely using fabric scissors.

 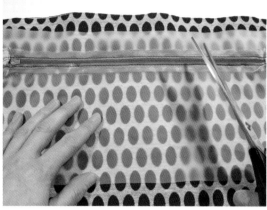

Repeat the last three steps for the lower plastic pocket: stitch, sew and trim, as illustrated.

Stick the edges of the back of the pocket to those of the top and lower pocket pieces using Copydex®. Wait for the glue to dry completely clear (overnight is best, since this is a bond between two nonporous plastic surfaces). Trim any edges straight that do not meet exactly flush when the glue is dry. Ensure the dimensions and proportions of the pockets are the same on both sides of the bag.

Stitch a 0.6 cm (¹/₄ in.) seam round the edge of the plastic pocket, on the wrong side, using the edge of the presser foot as a guide. Stitch through all layers of material in order to secure the pocket.

Stitch the top half of the bag outer to the lower half of the bag outer.

Topstitch this seam on the RS.

Pin an inner pattern piece to an outer pattern piece, around their top curves, with RSS (right sides) together, and sew along these pinned edges, leaving gaps for the carrying handle insertions, at the squared-off points.

Cut notches into the curves so the fabric will not pucker on the RS.

Turn the bag pieces RSS out. Topstitch the top curves.

Where the handle is to be inserted, turn the seams under. Insert one end of the handle, tack it in place, and then machine-sew securely to fix the handle.

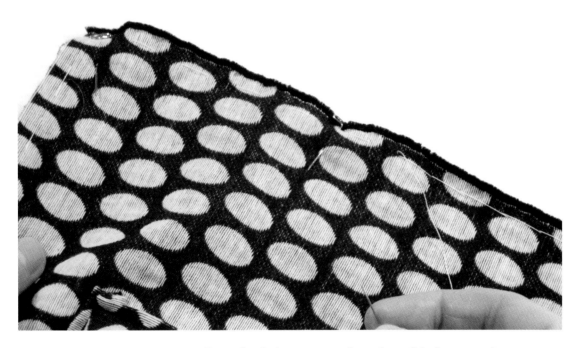

Pin and tack the remaining free edges of the bag outers/inners together to hold them fast. Then bring the RSS of the bag outers together. Tack all four layers together.

Sew all four layers together.

Zigzag stitch around the seam (through all four layers) to neaten it.
Turn the bag to its RS.

The finished bag.

5 pendant purse

With a 'tribal' or 'ethnic' feel, and incredibly easy to make in a weekend – though requiring a modicum of patience – this coin purse is made from two circles of leather sewn together and bound with a colourful silk Oriental-pattern ribbon binding. A loop of ribbon binding at the top allows a thong to be threaded through, by which the purse can be suspended from the neck or from a belt. A slot is cut in the leather back to accommodate a zip, whilst the front is decorated with a kaleidoscopic pattern of colourful rhinestones (this being the most arduous and time-consuming part). The simple circular purse design shows how the shape adapts exceptionally well to its function and how it can be easily transformed with carefully chosen decoration.

I do not provide quantities for the rhinestones needed; these can be counted out from the pattern. You may also want to reinterpret the pattern depending on the types of rhinestones you are able to obtain. The pattern is a kaleidoscopic one and will look good in a number of interpretations. It is always best to overbuy rhinestones in case they are lost from time to time. Hot-fix applicators for rhinestones are widely advertised but only work with the propri-etary rhinestones, and I find that the best method of fixing any type of rhinestone onto leather is with nail glue or superglue.

step-by-step method

Some materials you will need: silk ribbon binding, thread, nail glue, pins, tailor's chalk, rhinestones, tracing paper, cutting mat, leather, biro, steel rule, fineliner, scalpel.

YOU WILL NEED

▸ Cowhide leather pieces (for purse body), 0.15 cm (¹⁄₁₆ in.) thick

▸ 50 cm (20 in.) of 2.5 cm (1 in.) silk ribbon binding

▸ Leather thong

▸ Matching polyester thread

▸ Pins (for attaching rhinestones)

▸ Tailor's chalk (for transferring pattern)

▸ Fineliner pen

▸ Biro

▸ Steel rule

▸ Tracing paper

▸ Cutting mat

▸ Fabric scissors

▸ Scalpel

▸ Nail glue or superglue

▸ Rhinestones (for quantities see purse front pattern)

▸ Zip – longer than 7.5 cm (3 in.)

▸ Sewing machine with zipper foot, roller foot (optional)

For pattern see page 143.

Trace the designs for front and back.

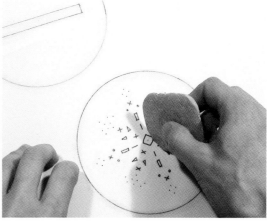

Turn the tracings over and cover their reverse sides with tailor's chalk.

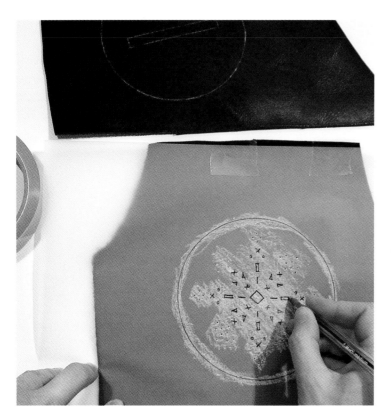

Tape the tracings chalked side down on top of the leather and trace the designs onto the leather using a biro.

Cut out the circles of leather making up the front and back of the purse using scissors.

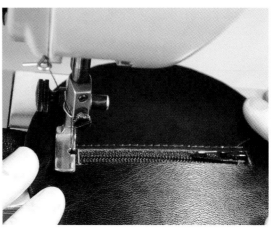

On the purse back, cut out the rectangular 7.5 cm (3 in.) slit for the zip neatly using a steel rule and sharp scalpel.

Position the zip so that the fly aligns with the top of the slit (this will hold the zip in place), and sew round it using a zipper foot.

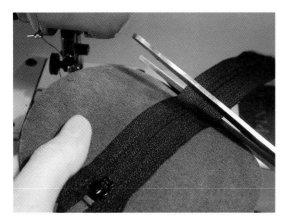

Turn the purse back over and cut the excess zip away.

Stitch the front and back of the purse together, WS to WS.

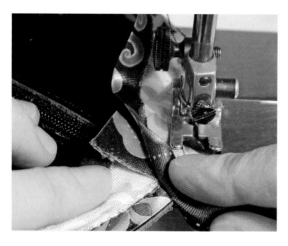

Stitch one side of the silk ribbon binding to the back of the purse, remembering to fold a section over at the beginning to make a neat finish, as illustrated.

Overlap the ends of the silk ribbon binding once the circle has been completed, and trim.

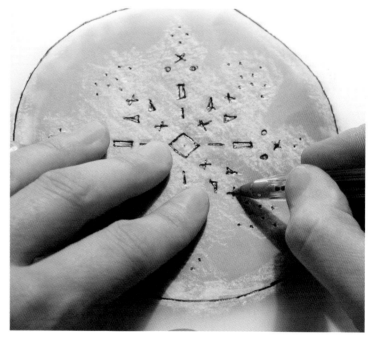

Pull the free side of the binding to the front side of the purse and stitch into position, ensuring that the binding simultaneously overlaps the stitching that joins the front and back sides of the purse and that the stitching remains the same distance from the edge of the binding on both sides.

At this stage you may want to touch up the chalk marks of the pattern on the front of the purse. Place the tracing paper over the leather in line with the original design and refresh the chalk marks by tracing.

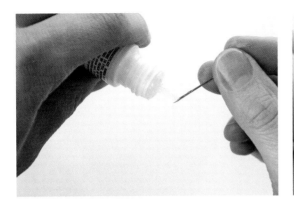
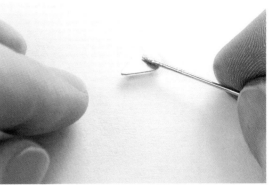

Now comes the fun part. Have your rhinestones at the ready! Squeeze out a drop or so of nail glue onto the end of a pin.

Spread the nail glue deftly over the back of a rhinestone.

Pick the rhinestone up, either with tweezers or a pin, and place it carefully and accurately on the leather base, following the pattern. Build up the pattern by working with one type of unit at a time (i.e. all brown oblongs or glass diamonds), and work from the inside to the outside.

This shows how two pins can be used to guide a rhinestone into position.

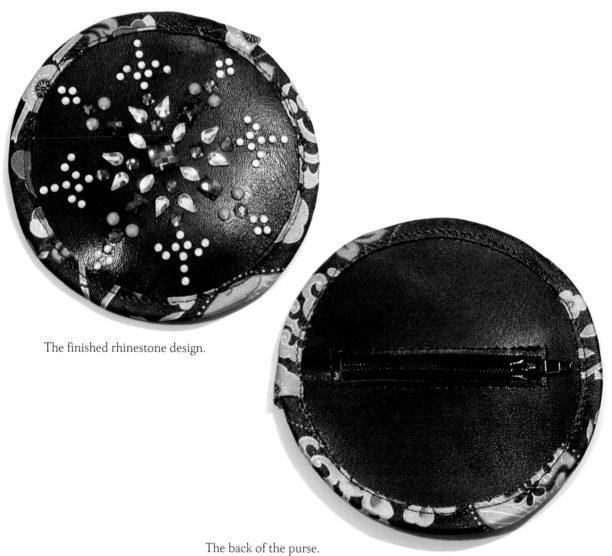

The finished rhinestone design.

The back of the purse.

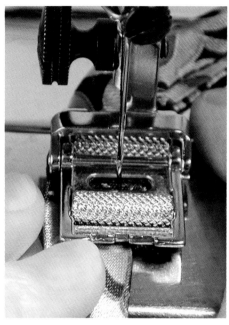

Cut a length of ribbon binding about 20 cm (8 in.) long.

Fold the ribbon binding in half along its length and sew along the edge. A roller foot may be beneficial, as the silk ribbon binding when sewn without support can be quite delicate and prone to snags.

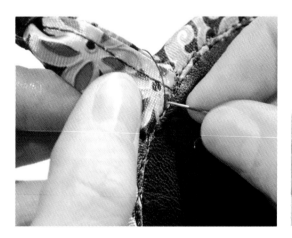

Make a loop by folding under one end of the length of stitched ribbon and sew it, using handstitching, to the inner edge of the front of the purse. Tie a knot that falls in the middle of the ribbon length. Fold the remaining end of the length under and handstitch it to the inner edge of the back of the purse.

Catch the sides of the ribbon loop with a couple of handstitches on each side.

The finished purse (front).

6 exotic fabrics bag

Fabulous and unusual contrasting fabrics combine in this lined soft, 'girly' bag, which looks complicated but is actually astonishingly simple to make. The top half of the bag consists of a padded section made from a beautiful piece of authentic Japanese-print cotton which was given to me. This is given added bulk with fusible wadding so that the upper half of the bag has stability, and is quilted to follow the shape of the curved pattern pieces, which overlap each other.

The bottom half of the bag is made from a gathered remnant of gold and black lamé, which was simply too good to pass up! This demonstrates how fabrics which are radically different from each other can be combined successfully with a little imagination.

The join between the fabrics is concealed by a length of double-faced satin ribbon chosen to harmonize with the fabrics. The same double-faced ribbon is also used to make the carrying straps, which are further accessorized and strengthened by circular metal hoops.

Observe how the various design elements offset, contrast or harmonize with each other and how balance in the design is achieved by adding just enough of each coloured element or notion (for example fabrics, ribbons or notions). Try to mirror the qualities of your chosen fabrics in the notions and trimmings you choose.

The bag was lined with a striking shot red/green acetate lining, appropriate when it is borne in mind that the combination of gold (yellow) and blue (navy) is green. This may seem like a strange rationalisation, but it actually works! There is no method of closure to this bag.

step-by-step method

Some of the materials you will need: lining, lamé fabric, Japanese printed cotton fabric, wadding, matching thread, tacking thread, tailor's chalk, rings, ribbon.

YOU WILL NEED

- Printed cotton
- Lighter fabric, i.e. light- to medium-weight lamé
- Shot acetate lining
- Wadding (Vilene® H640)
- 285 cm (3 ¹/₉ yds) of 1.3 cm (¹/₂ in.) double-faced satin ribbon

- Matching polyester thread
- Tacking thread
- Needle
- Pins
- Tailor's chalk
- White pencil
- Ordinary drawing pencil

- Fineliner
- Fabric scissors
- 4 2.5 cm (1 in.) round rings (for handle attachments)
- Sewing machine with zipper foot

For pattern see page 144.

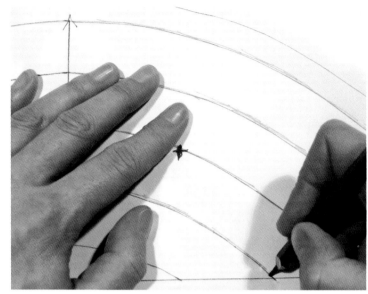

Chalk the backs of both pieces of paper making up the bag top pattern with tailor's chalk. Place the paper patterns on your chosen fabric WS down.

Trace the lines of the quilting pattern onto the fabric using a pencil.

Heighten quilting lines and crosses showing positions of the carrying straps in white pencil if necessary.

Trace round the bag top patterns onto the reverse (glue) side of the wadding using a fineliner.

Stitch the tops of the outer fabric pattern pieces, making up the top of the bag together.

Trim off 0.6 cm (¹/₄ in.) all round the drawn pattern pieces on the wadding.

Cut out, tack and stitch the acetate lining pieces together along their side edges.

Pin and stitch the lamé pieces, which will form the lower half of the bag, together along their sides.

Iron one side (WS) of the fabric making up the bag top, onto the wadding, then turn it RS out, so that it encloses the wadding and forms half of the bag top, ready for quilting.

Quilt along the quilting lines drawn on the RS of the material. I used a quilting attachment – part of the equipment that came with my machine – for optimum accuracy. This can be adjusted to fit the desired spacing of quilting lines; I chose a 2.5 cm (1 in.) spacing between the lines. If you do not have such an attachment, follow your chalked lines carefully and make sure the lines are as equidistant as possible.

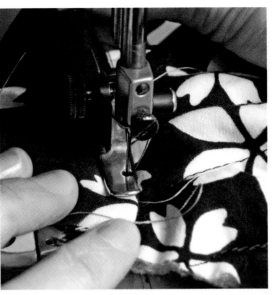

Sandwich side B in between the outer and inner fabric sections of side A, and tack (leave the lower edge of both sides free).

Stitch the joins between side A and B close to their edges, using a zipper foot. Stitch through all layers to secure the sides to each other. Each side of the bag top should be a mirror-image of the other.

Trim off any excess material at the lower edge of the bag top.

Using a double thread, tack and gather 2.5 cm (1 in.) from the top of the lamé fabric.

Pin and tack the quilted section to the gathered section.

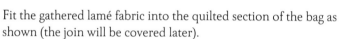

Fit the gathered lamé fabric into the quilted section of the bag as shown (the join will be covered later).

Sew the quilted section to the gathered section.

Tack and handsew double-faced satin ribbon over the join between both sections to cover it. Handsew along both edges of the ribbon using small imperceptible stitches.

Pull the lining over the gathered section and tack it to the quilted section concealing the join between the cotton and lamé fabrics. Turn the edge of the lining under as you go. Then hand-stitch the lining to the quilted section using hemstitching.

Turn the bag inside out.

The bag, inside out.

Cut 4 x 10 cm (4 in.) pieces of ribbon.

Fold double one of the pieces of ribbon and thread it on to a ring so that it is positioned at the 'folded' end. Sew across the ribbon close to the ring using a zipper foot to secure it.

Fold under the free ends of the ribbon, which will form the carrying strap base, and sew through all ribbon and bag layers to one of the crosses marking the position of the carrying straps. Repeat this and the last two steps for all remaining rings and 10 cm (4 in.) pieces of ribbon.

Cut 2 x 1m (40 in.) pieces of ribbon. Loop ribbon through the rings on either side, double them and bring them together to make a carrying strap.

Working on one side at a time, fold one end of the ribbon under to neaten it, and tack through all ribbon layers to secure them. Make sure that the lengths of the ribbons are equal on both sides.

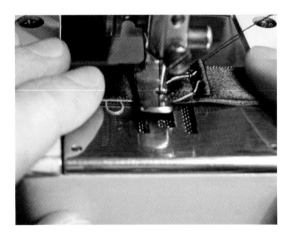

Stitch the ribbon layers into position using a zipper foot and two seams running parallel to each other across the ribbon, to make a carrying strap. Repeat for the second carrying strap.

Stitch the carrying strap close to the ring to secure it.

The finished bag.

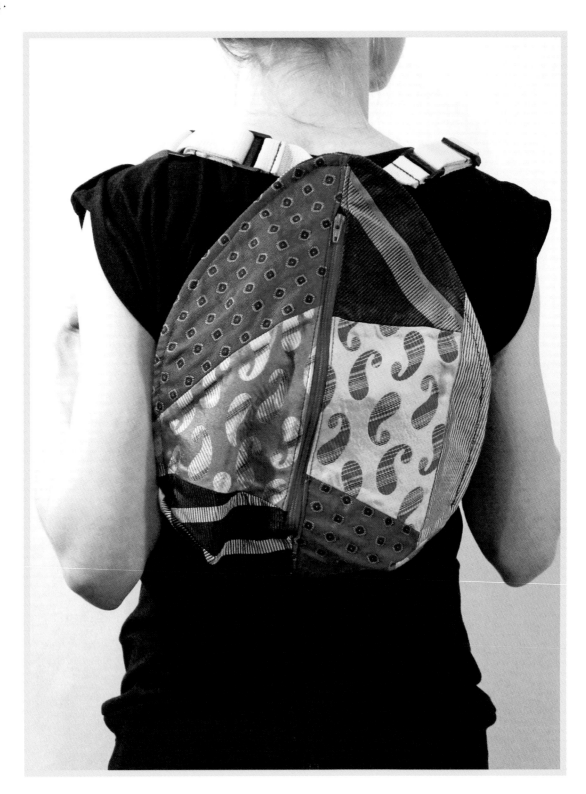

7 patchwork mini-rucksack

This small and rather gorgeous patch-work mini-rucksack is made from tie silks. It is child-sized, but the pattern can be scaled up to one-and-a-half or twice the size to make a larger and roomier adult-sized bag. The child-sized version is in any event large enough to carry a packet of sandwiches, apple, and small notebook.

Carefully selected silk patchwork pieces are stitched together and mounted on pieces of fusible drill to match the main bag pattern pieces. If you look closely you'll see that the base and zipped front of the bag are actually continuous. This is a way of creating a bag base without having to make a separate piece and reduces the amount of stitching and piecing (which, for a bag base, may be time-consuming). It also makes the process of pattern making a little more interesting.

The carrying straps are made from brightly coloured polypropylene, to harmo-nize with the general 'mood' of the rest of the bag, and finished with navy blue plastic buckles, again to harmonize with the colour scheme. They are adjustable and stitched to the main bag body using a decorative 'cross-in-box' stitching pattern. The bag is fully lined and the upper edge topstitched to define its shape.

NB In the demonstration photographs I have used silver metal buckles and D-rings, which in themselves show one way of con-structing the bag strap. However, I subse-quently came across some navy plastic buck-les which were far more in tune with the style and general appearance of the bag. I was able to substitute these easily for the original buckles and D-rings as the carrying straps are made in two parts; I simply unpicked the buckle ends of the carrying straps, placed the new buckles at the desired position and re-sewed the seams.

step-by-step method

Some materials you will need: tie silks, fusible drill, lining, zip, matching thread, tacking thread, polypropylene webbing, buckles.

YOU WILL NEED

- Tie silks or other stable medium-weight materials of various colours
- Fusible drill
- Acetate lining
- Matching polyester thread

- Tacking thread (silk)
- Needle
- White pencil
- Fineliner
- Fabric scissors

- 182 cm (2 yds) of 2.5 cm (1 in.) polypropylene webbing
- Either: 2 x 2.5 cm (1 in.) buckles and 2 x D-rings, or 4 x 2.5 cm (1 in.) buckles
- Sewing machine with zipper foot

For pattern see page 145.

Mark the fusible drill using a fineliner and cut around it.

Cut out the lining fabric pieces using the main bag pattern.

Machine-patchwork pieces of tie silk together so that the eventual patchworked piece of fabric will fit the bag pattern shapes. Press the seams open as you go along.

Iron the fusible drill pieces onto the pieces of patchworked tie silk.

Cut the edges of the tie silk flush with the drill.

Cut pieces of spare fabric 2.5 cm (1 in.) wide and 10 cm (4 in.) long to cover the zip ends. Tack and sew them to the zip ends.

Tack and sew the zip onto the bag outer in line with the notches that mark its ends, using a zipper foot.

Tack and sew the rest of the bag side/base, to which the zipper does not extend, using a zipper foot.

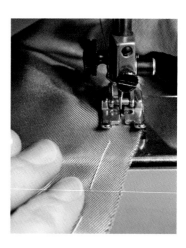

Stitch the linings, leaving a gap in the centre for the zip opening.

To make doubly sure the seam is flat, press it open on the WS of the bag outer.

Press the seam adjacent to the zip flat from the RS, using a medium setting.

Topstitch the seam closely on the RS using a zipper foot.

Stitch the side darts up – these will form the base of the bag.

Place the paper pattern over the bag back. Mark the positions of the carrying straps with white pencil through holes in the pattern.

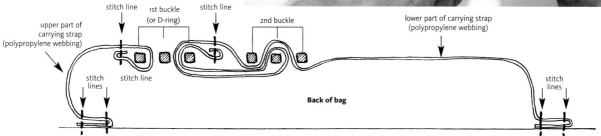

upper part of carrying strap (polypropylene webbing)

stitch line · 1st buckle (or D-ring) · stitch line · 2nd buckle · lower part of carrying strap (polypropylene webbing)

stitch lines · stitch line · stitch lines

Back of bag

Scheme of attaching/threading carrying straps through buckles or D-rings (not to scale).

Cut 1 x 15 cm (6 in.) length of polypropylene webbing and 1 x 63 cm (25 in.) length. Thread one end of the 15 cm (6 in.) length of webbing through one side of a D-ring or buckle, fold it back on itself and turn the end under. Then thread the longer length of webbing through the opposite side of the D-ring or buckle and fold it back on itself, before passing the webbing through the centre of a second buckle. Again fold the webbing back on itself and pass again through the first buckle or D-ring so that it overlies the first run of polypropylene webbing. Pass it again through the centre of the second buckle, and allow it to continue to the position at the bag base where it will be secured. The remaining free end of the longer part of the carrying strap at the buckle end should be turned under and sewn to the overlying webbing to secure it, so that the carrying strap will become adjustable. Tack the turned-under fold to secure it. Repeat on the opposite side.

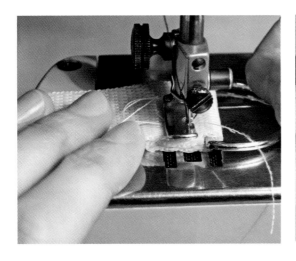

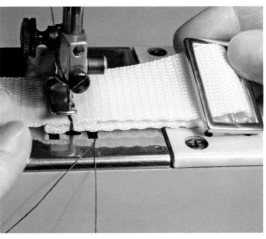

Stitch the fold of the D-ring (or buckle) down using a contrast thread. Stitch backwards and forwards along the seam 5 or 6 times.

Do the same for the buckle; it will not need to be so closely secured. Repeat the last 3 steps for the other carrying strap.

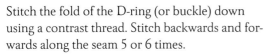

Fold the free ends of the upper carrying straps over and tack them, so that their edges are level with each other, at the centrally marked point on the upper back of the piece. Position these sections of the carrying straps so that the folds will eventually face downwards. Stitch them into position using a 'box and cross' stitching pattern (as indicated). Sew about 3 times over all seams.

Fold the ends of the lower section of the carrying straps under in the same way, so that the folds will eventually point downwards. Tack them at the points marked by crosses on the lower part of the back section. Secure them with a 'box and cross' stitching pattern as indicated.

The back of the bag is now complete.

The front of the bag.

Stitch the back and front of the bag together to make the outer shell.

Insert the lining into the outer shell. Turning the edges of the lining under as you go, join the zip to the lining with tacking and tiny hemstitches about 1.3 cm ($^{1}/_{2}$ in.) – 0.6 cm ($^{1}/_{4}$ in.) from the zip teeth, so that the zip does not catch the lining. As a finishing touch, topstitch the upper section of the bag 0.6 cm ($^{1}/_{4}$ in.) from its edge, using a zipper foot. End the lines of stitching about 2.5 cm (1 in.) from each lower corner.

(**opposite**) The completed bag.

8 faux fur shoulder bag

Made from a fun, textured, lightweight faux fur fabric, the design of this large shoulder bag may actually be appealing to both sexes, and makes rather a good 'man-bag'. The bag is edged with red bias binding and features a jazzy red contrast acetate lining and carrying strap of black polypropylene. It fastens with a strip of Velcro® on the underside of the front flap, and is roomy enough to carry A4 documents and files.

Don't feel restricted to the fabrics shown; this bag can also look good in canvas, dense wool or felt, denim, or leatherette, with the procedure obviously varying depending on the fabric chosen. The pattern is a simple one; the front and back of the bag are formed from the same piece of fabric, and the bag sides form the gusset.

step-by-step method

Some of the materials you may need: faux fur fabric, fusible drill, Velcro®, tacking thread, matching thread, binding, polypropylene webbing, fineliner.

YOU WILL NEED

- Lightweight faux fur fabric
- Fusible drill
- Matching polyester thread
- Tacking thread
- Needle
- Pins

- Fineliner
- 252 cm (2¾ yds) of 1.9 cm (¾ in.) width bias binding
- 107 cm (1¹/₆ yds) of 3.8 cm (1½ in.) polypropylene webbing

- 33 cm (13 in.) strip of 5 cm (2 in.) Velcro®
- Fabric scissors
- Sewing machine with zipper foot

For pattern see page 146.

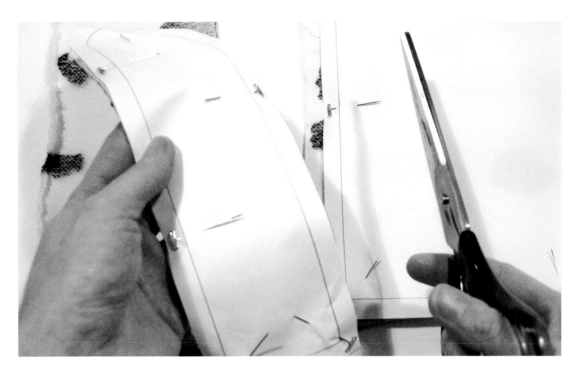

Cut out the faux fur pieces.

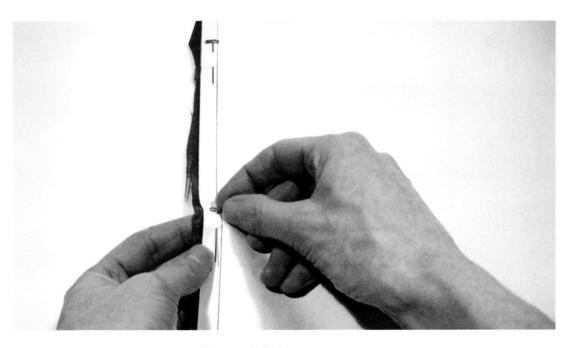

Cut out the lining.

Cut out the fusible drill. Cut 0.3 cm (⅛ in.) inside the marked edge.

Draw round the pattern pieces onto the fusible drill with a fineliner.

Iron the fusible drill onto the faux fur, working on the drill side of the composite fabric.

Tack the faux fur sections to their corresponding lining sections.

Tack and sew the side pieces of the bag to the main bag body.

Bind the top edges, then the side edges of the bag; cut separate binding pieces for each edge.

The bag prior to binding.

'Cross-in-box' pattern of stitching

Tack each end of the length of polypropylene carrying strap to the bag side, folding it back on itself to neaten; the fold should point downwards.

Stitch the ends of the carrying strap into position using a box-in-cross stitching pattern as indicated. Go over all seams at least 3 times.

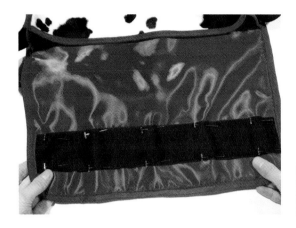

Pin one half of the Velcro® (hooked part) to the underside of the top flap of the bag, about 2.5 cm (1 in.) from the bound edge.

Handstitch the Velcro® to the top flap using tiny imperceptible hemstitches.

Pin the other half of the Velcro® (fuzzy part) in a corresponding position on the front panel of the bag – about 7.9 cm (3¼ in.) down from the top flap edge (see above). Then, handstitch the Velcro® into position.

The finished bag.

9 feather purse

A 'red-carpet' item, this feathered and bead-embroidered purse is made using a simple base constructed of circles of silk, acetate lining and wadding. A semicircle of iridescent green cock-feather trim and overlapping large sequins are then attached, with large sew-on jewels and iridescent, harmonising purple, green and blue seed beads filling in the background of the upper purse body. Finally, the purse body is fixed into the purse clasp carefully using nail glue or superglue.

It is essential to get a good blend of decorative elements, since the success of this piece depends mainly upon its applied surface decoration. Take some time to find a good, rich and harmonious balance of colours and textures. Again, don't necessarily feel restricted to what is shown in the book, but work out your own scheme of decoration.

step-by-step method

Some materials you will need: silk fabric, lining, purse frame, nail glue, PVA, sewing thread, needle, brush, iridescent beads, beading needles, feathers, sew-on jewels, large sequins.

YOU WILL NEED

- Silk fabric
- Acetate lining
- 30 cm (12 in.) – 17.5 cm (7 in.) iridescent cock-feather trim
- Matching silk threads
- Needle

- Beading needle
- Fabric scissors
- Old brush
- PVA glue
- Nail glue or superglue
- 20 large sew-on jewels

- Packet large 2.5 cm (1 in.) diameter sequins
- Iridescent seed/bugle beads
- Purse frame, semicircular, 12.7 cm (5 in.) diameter

For pattern see pages 147.

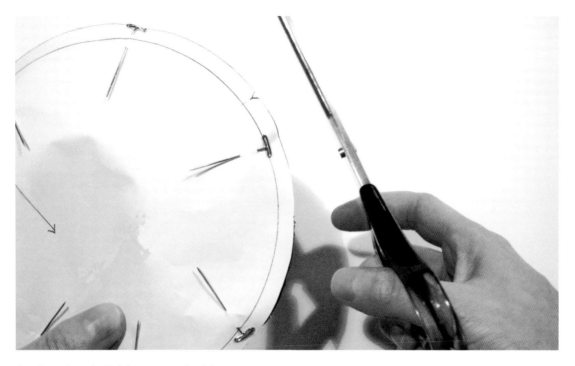

Cut 2 circles of silk fabric using the fabric pattern.

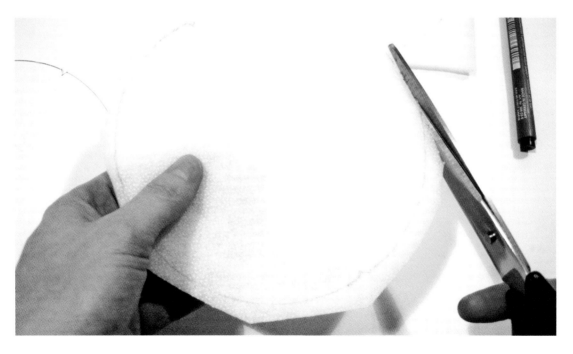

Mark 2 circles of wadding with the fineliner using the fabric pattern, and cut out.

Iron the silk onto the wadding.

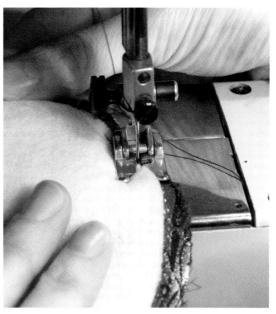

Stitch the 2 outers of the purse RSS together.

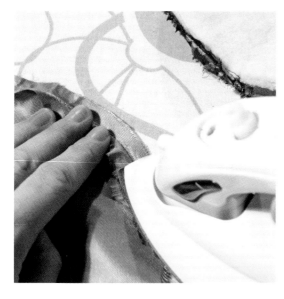

Stitch the linings together and press the seams folding them back on themselves, so that they will lie flat against the outer.

Place the silk outer inside the lining so that the RSS of both fabrics face each other. Sew one side of the outer to the corresponding side of the lining.

Turn the purse to its RS.

Check that the purse body fits the purse frame at this stage.

Handsew the other side of the purse, turning under and joining the edges of the silk and lining materials as you go.

Topstitch all around the upper edge of the purse.

On both sides, make a line of tacking on the lower half of the purse, 3.8 cm (1¹/₂ in.) from the edge.

Tack the feather trim along the tacked line.

Cut a length of feather trim to fit along this line.

Using matching thread, stitch the trim along the tacked line along both its upper and lower edges.

Sew large sew-on jewels to the top of the purse to create the basic structure for the bead embroidery.

Sew large sequins to the lower half of the purse, working upwards from the edge of the feather trim. Ensure that the sequins overlap each other (work from the bottom upwards) and that they cover the edge of the feather trim.

Fill in the gaps between the large sew-on rhinestones using a beading needle with iridescent seed and bugle beads.

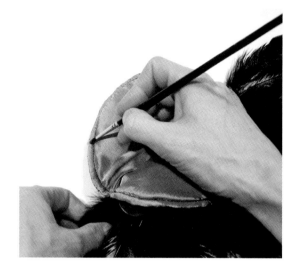

Coat the top edge of the purse with a thin film of PVA glue and leave to dry thoroughly. This will ensure that the nail glue adheres properly when you come to apply it, as it gives the fabric some grip. Be careful not to let the glue touch any other area of the fabric.

Apply nail glue to the inside of the purse frame. (Work on one side of the purse frame at a time.)

Insert one of the top edges of the purse into the purse frame. Hold the purse frame so that it points downwards and keep it propped in this position for a while. This will ensure the best adhesion. Work on one side of the purse frame at a time.

The finished purse.

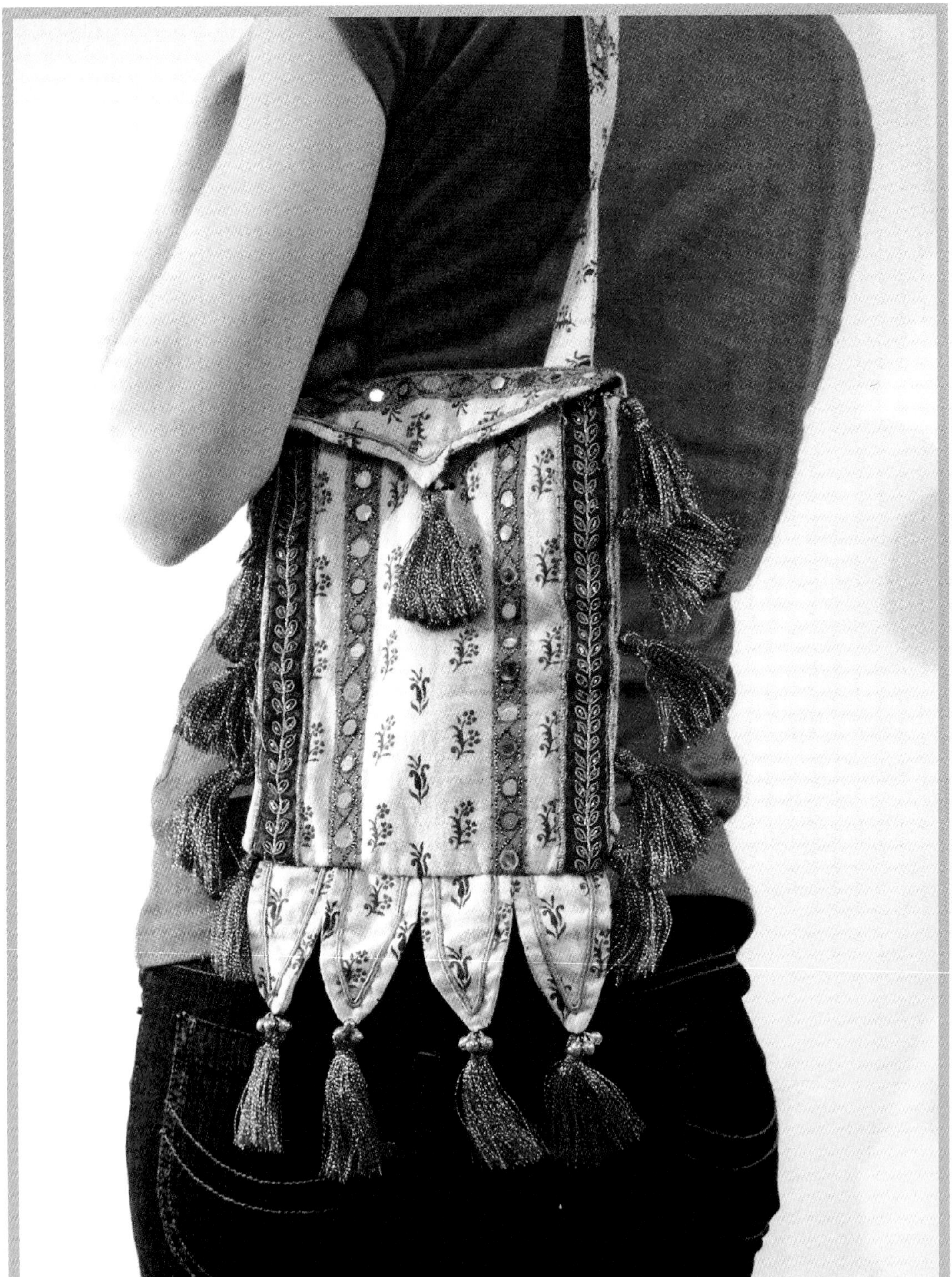

10 indian bag

This is a very popular design, perhaps because of its unusual Indian-inspired 'ethnic' flavour. It uses genuine Indian cottons and vintage trims (including a shisha mirror trim), along with a thin printed paisley silk lining, harmonizing lurex tassels, thin gold furnishing braid and tiny gold effect bells to finish.

The tricky parts to this bag are perhaps sewing the ogee-shaped flap and the arrowhead-shaped decorative elements at the base of the bag. In all other respects the bag is fairly straightforward to construct. It is slightly stiffened with a light but firm fusible stiffener, as the cotton itself is fairly lightweight. Both hand and machine construction are used here. Quite a lot of handstitch-ing is used to sew on the trims and this may take some time.

The printing on Indian fabrics of this type may very often be directional. Where this is the case, as for the fabric used in this project, ensure that the pattern pieces are cut so that the print proceeds the right way up the fabric. It does not matter that the bag flap at the top, which is a continuation from the bag back, will show the design going 'the wrong way' since a relatively small amount of the fabric is on show. However, the bag back, front, and tabs all need to be cut with respect to the direction of pattern.

The bag carrying strap does not have a pattern provided. It can be drawn directly onto the fabric.

step-by-step method

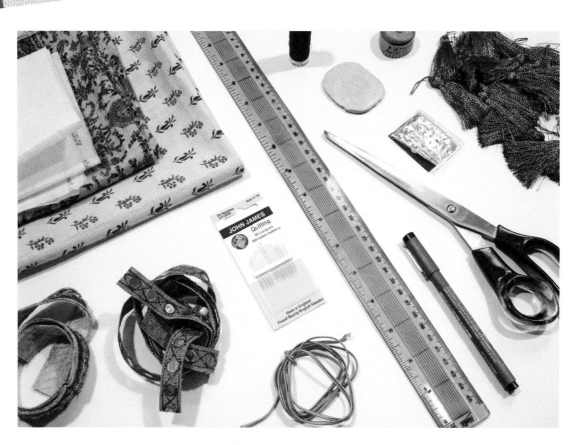

Materials you may need: Indian cotton fabric, silk Indian printed lining fabric, thin firm fusible, Indian metallic and shisha mirror trims, needles, contrast thread, tailor's chalk, bells, lurex tassels, ruler, fineliner.

YOU WILL NEED

- Printed Indian cotton fabric
- Thin silk fabric for lining (not silk satin)
- Vilene® H250
- 41 cm (16 in.) of 2 cm (1 in.) Indian metallic trim
- 59 cm (23 in.) of 1.6 cm (⅝ in.) Indian shisha mirror trim

- 66 cm (26 in.) of 0.3 cm (⅛ in.) furnishing braid
- Contrast polyester thread
- Needle
- Tailor's chalk
- Fineliner
- Ruler

- 20 x 6.3 cm (2½ in.) lurex tassels
- 27 x small 0.6cm (¼ in.) diameter bells
- Small hook and eye
- Sewing machine with zipper foot

For pattern see page 148.

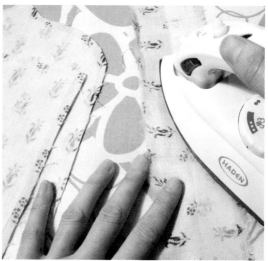

Mark out all fabric pieces, including the fusible, using the bag pattern as a template. Trim the fusible 0.3 cm (¹/₈ in.) inside all drawn edges – this will avoid bulking out of the seams later on. To make the carrying strap, use your ruler and fineliner pen to mark a strip measuring 71 cm (28 in.) x 6.3 cm (2¹/₂ in.) onto the printed fabric, and also a strip measuring 71 cm (28 in.) x 2.5 cm (1 in.) onto the fusible.

Iron the fusible to all pieces, including one side of the carrying strap; the outer edge of the fusible should be about 0.6 cm (¹/₄ in.) inside one of the long outer edges of the printed fabric.

Sew a tassel to the point of one of the arrowhead pieces as illustrated, on the RS.

Place another arrowhead piece over the top of the tassel and stitch the arrowhead closed using a zipper foot, in the manner illustrated.

Turn the arrowhead right side
out and press.

Topstitch the arrowhead 0.6 cm (¹/₄ in.)from its edge using a contrast
thread. Make four arrowheads in total, following the same method.

Stitch five tassels along the centre of the carrying
strap as shown, spacing them equidistantly from
each other, so that they will mark the top of the
shoulder. Fold the carrying strap in half; fold the
long edges under about 0.6 cm (¹/₄ in.)and press.

Tack the long free sides of the carrying strap
together, then handstitch the seam using tiny oversewing stitches.

Cut the trims to fit across the front and back bag sections and carrying strap. Tack them into position. Handstitch tassels to the back long section as shown on page 96.

Sew the trims onto the fabric using imperceptible handstitching.

Cut furnishing braid to cover the topstitched seams on the front parts of the arrowheads, and tack into position.

Secure the braid using tiny imperceptible stitches.

Tack the ends of the carrying strap onto the bag back into a position about 2.5 cm (1 in.) from each side of the bag and 0.6 cm ($^1/_4$ in.) from its top. Then sew the ends on to the bag back using a zipper foot, close to the edge, in a 'box' stitching pattern (as shown).

Tack the arrowheads in position on the outside of the bag back (as shown), so that the sides decorated with furnishing braid will eventually face the front.

Tack the front and back of both the bag outer and bag lining together.

Sew up the bag outer and lining side seams. You may need to secure the tassel bases about 0.6 cm ($^1/_4$ in.) inside the bag outer seams with a few catch stitches in order to anchor them fully.

Insert the outer of the bag inside the lining.

Tack the silk lining to the upper edge of the bag, leaving a gap in the bag front for the bag to be turned to its RS. Sew the tacked upper edge (as illustrated). Then turn the bag RS out and press the sewn upper edge.

Stitch the seam of the top edge of the bag front to the lining with tiny imperceptible stitches.

Sew groups of 2–3 bells at the bases of the tassels, where they meet the fabric.

Sew the parts of a hook and eye onto the top centre of the front panel and at the inner tip of the ogee formed by the back panel.

The finished bag.

11 city bag

This is a squashy, roomy bag made from medium weight denim that coordinates well with most smart-casual wear; in fact, I use this bag a lot myself, as it matches with just about everything. Inside, the bag is given a slightly updated feel with a mesh lining, mobile phone/purse compartment and larger pocket with elasticated upper edge which can accommodate an extra pair of shoes or vest and tracksuit bottoms for the gym (this has been tried and tested with success).

The bag is given a 'designer' touch by means of large decorative buttons covering the points of attachment of the handles to the bag body. Choose the most sophisticated-looking buttons you can get for this purpose, with a classical feel; if possible, buttons that don't actually look like buttons, to avoid a 'handcraft' look for this bag.

The bag handles are strengthened by means of two rows of piping cord sandwiched inside the handles, which also gives an interesting texture and good grip. There is no pattern for the handles; these can be marked out directly onto the fabric using a ruler and set square.

step-by-step method

Some materials you will need: large buttons, denim, black mesh fabric (for lining), matching thread, tacking thread, piping cord, magnetic fastener, ruler, set square.

YOU WILL NEED

▶ Medium weight denim

▶ Black mesh fabric with a slight stretch (this does not matter), for lining

▶ 41 cm (16 in.) of 1.5 cm (½ in.) black elastic

▶ 230 cm (2½ yds) of 0.6 cm (¼ in.) piping cord

▶ Matching polyester thread

▶ Tacking thread (contrast colour)

▶ Needle

▶ Pins

▶ White pencil

▶ Ruler

▶ Set square

▶ Fabric scissors

▶ Miniature pliers

▶ Magnetic fastener 1.9 cm (¾ in.) diameter

▶ 4 large buttons, 3.8 cm (1½ in.) diameter

▶ Sewing machine with zipper foot

For pattern see pages 149-151.

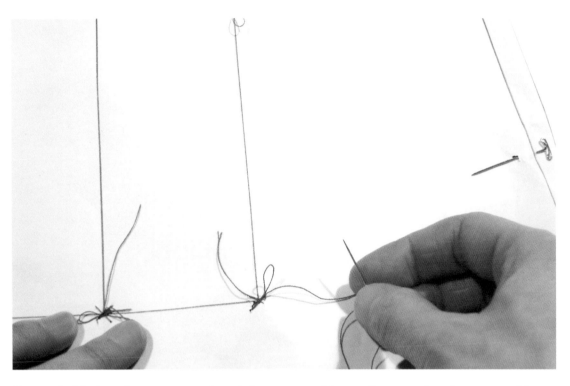

Cut out the black net lining pieces and mark the position of the smaller internal pocket on one of them, using crossed contrast tacking stitches through the pattern paper.

Remove the pattern paper from the net. The positions of the pocket corners should be visibly marked through the tacking stitches.

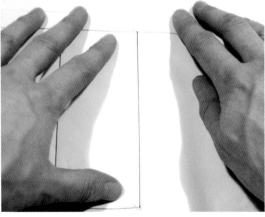

Fold the edge of the lining pattern piece down along the indicated line to make the pattern for the large inside pocket.

Cut the small and large pocket
pieces from the net, and the bag
shell and inside facing from the
denim. Mark the positions of
the handles with white pencil.

Tack the facings to the upper
edges of each bag side, and
make tucks as indicated
between pairs of notches at the
bag base. Secure these with
tacking.

Stitch the tucks and facing into position.

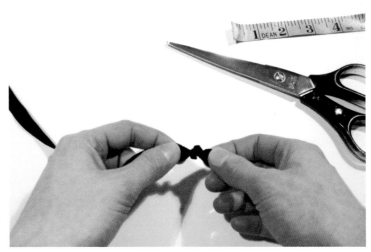

Turn under the top of the large net pocket about 1.3 cm ($^1/_2$ in.) and stitch.

Make a knot in both ends of the black elastic.

Draw the elastic through the channel formed by the turned-under top of the net pocket, and secure it at both ends with tacking stitches.

Stitch both ends of the elasticated pocket to secure the elastic. Go backwards and forwards a few times, using a zipper foot.

Trim the knots off using scissors.

Turn under the edges of the combination pocket 0.6 cm ($^1/_4$ in.) and stitch using a zipper foot.

Stitch both sides of the bag shell together, RS to RS.

Tack the combination pocket piece, where indicated, on one of the inner lining pieces.

Tack the large elasticated pocket to the other inner lining piece.

Stitch the smaller combination pocket to its corresponding lining piece. Stitch the divider between the pockets first, then fold the inner notches of the mobile phone pocket towards its outer corners so that the pocket is shaped. Secure the folds with tacking stitches prior to sewing. This shaping will ensure that the mobile does not 'escape' from the pocket!

Stitch the large elasticated pocket to the inner lining.

Stitch the lining pieces together along their side edges, RS to RS. Do not stitch the top edge. Leave a generous gap in the base through which the bag will later be turned. Then turn the bag facings over the top edge of the bag so their WS shows. Turn the lining so its WS faces outwards, then place the bag shell inside it and tack the top edge of the lining to the lower edge of the WS of the bag facing, as shown.

Stitch the lining edge and facing together.

Turn the bag and lining to their RSS through the gap in the lining and press down the facing.

Topstitch the top edge of the bag about 1.3 cm (¹/₂ in.) from the edge using a zipper foot, to secure the facing.

The bag so far, minus handles.

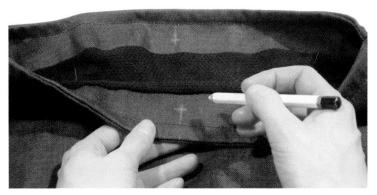

Mark the positions for the magnetic clasp parts in the centre of each bag side. These must match each other perfectly. Use a tape-measure and folding to centre the positions.

Using the gap in the lining to help you, fix the parts of the magnetic clasp to the back of the facing using miniature pliers.

Use handstitching to stitch up the gap in the lining, using imperceptible stitches.

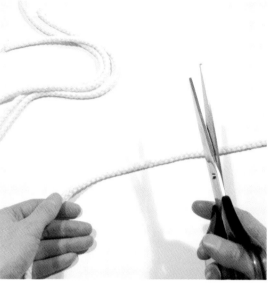

To make the bag handles, cut 2 long strips of denim, 10 cm (4 in.) by 64 cm (25 in.).

Cut 4 lengths of piping cord, each 56 cm (22 in.) long.

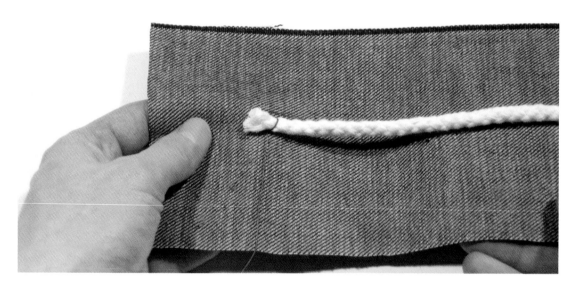

Tack the end of one of the pieces of piping cord to the centre of one of the strips, about 5 cm (2 in.) from the end, to hold it in position.

Using a zipper foot, make a seam to encase the piping cord in the centre of the denim strip.

Do the same for another length of piping cord, placing it parallel to the first.

Trim off any excess piping cord at the ends of the bag carrying strap. Then stitch across the width of the strap, where the piping cords end, to secure them. Ensure, before you do this, that the lengths of piping cord are the same on both sides.

Turn under the free, long edges of the bag strap and pin/tack.

Topstitch the edge of the bag strap, very close to the edge, using a zipper foot.

Tack the bag straps in position on the bag at the points where the piping cord ends, folding under the ends to neaten. The fact that piping cord is not present in these areas will make your job easier, though you will still, at this stage, be sewing through several thicknesses of denim.

Finish the bag by adding large decorative buttons to cover the point of attachment of the bag straps.

Using a zipper foot, stitch the bag straps onto the bag.

The finished bag.

12 butterfly bag

Though you might not have realised it, this bag uses exactly the same canvas fabric as in the Canvas Bag in Chapter 3. It's a good example of how you can effectively use up a quantity of fabric in making different items, rather than being left with large lengths of unused fabric.

The front of the bag incorporates a large appliqué and embroidered butterfly design, which is outlined in contrast white top-stitching. Parts of the pattern are appliquéd using different coloured leathers cut from suede ribbons, leather offcuts and second-hand leather garments, and additional decoration is provided with bead and sequin embroidery. The carrying handle is made from a piece of furnishing cord twisted and knotted around itself and drawn through large eyelets fixed at the uppermost points of the bag. The bag is unlined and fastens with a zip at the top edge. It's a fun, cheerful, jazzy sort of a bag that will accommodate the usual purse, makeup, hairbrush etc.

The pattern is provided at life-size on pages 152-155, in four parts. Trace this onto taped-together sheets of layout paper or tracing paper, ready to transfer onto the bag front.

This bag actually provides a good incentive to collect fabrics and materials that give the best and most harmonious interpretation of the design possible. Take time to collect fabrics for the bag and to make it, or ransack your fabrics chest and use up oddments that are languishing doing nothing!

step-by-step method

Some materials you will need: PVA glue, canvas, tracing paper, thread, tacking thread, sequins, tailor's chalk, beads, beading needles, needle, eyelets, hammer, brush, zip, pencil, cord, coloured leather, suede ribbon.

YOU WILL NEED

- Canvas
- Different coloured leathers (from offcuts, old leather garments, etc.)
- Suede ribbon
- 152 cm (60 in.) of 0.6 cm (¼ in.) diameter furnishing cord
- Matching/contrasting polyester thread
- Tacking thread

- Needle
- Pins
- Beading needle
- Propelling pencil or ordinary drawing pencil
- White pencil
- Fineliner pen
- Tailor's chalk
- Tracing paper

- Fabric scissors
- Hammer
- Old brush
- PVA glue
- Coloured sequins
- Iridescent glass beads
- 2 x 11 mm (7/16 in.) diameter eyelets
- Zip, to harmonize, 23 cm (9 in.)

For pattern see pages 152-155.

Chalk the back of the paper pattern using tailor's chalk.

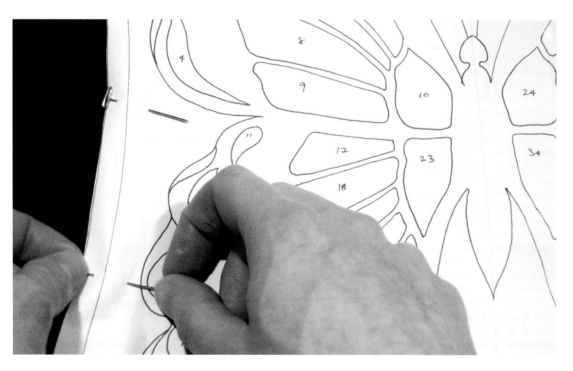

Pin the pattern to the canvas, chalk side down.

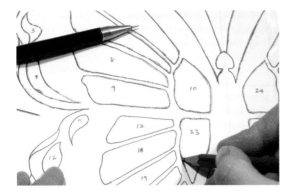

Using a propelling pencil or ordinary drawing
pencil, trace the pattern onto the canvas.

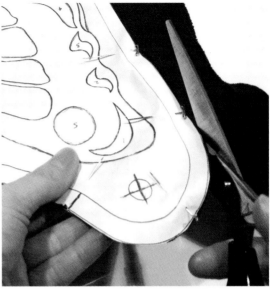

Cut out the canvas, which will make the bag base.

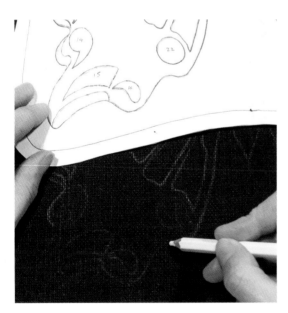

Heighten any chalk marks that may be indistinct
with a white pencil.

Topstitch round the outside of the butterfly motif
with a double line of stitching.

Mark the zip and eyelet points at the top of the bag in white pencil.

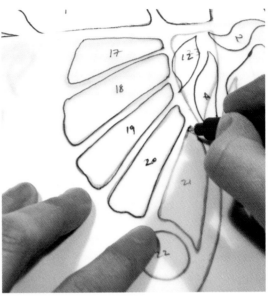

From the paper pattern, trace the numbered sections of the design onto tracing paper using a fineliner pen. Number the sections on the tracing paper.

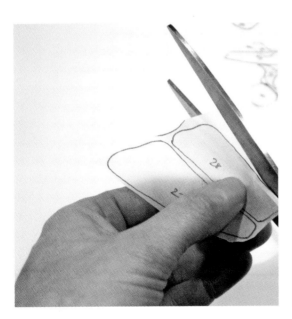

Cut the pieces of tracing paper out with paper scissors.

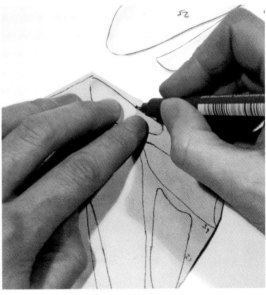

Using the fineliner, trace round the pieces of tracing paper onto pieces of coloured leather. Write the number of each pattern piece by its side.

Using an old brush, stick the pieces of leather into their marked positions on the canvas with PVA glue, working one colour at a time to avoid confusion and cutting and sticking pieces one by one to be sure of their number and position.

All the pieces in position.

Machine-appliqué all the pieces to the canvas, stitching close to the edges.

Zigzag round the edge of the canvas to neaten it and prevent fraying.

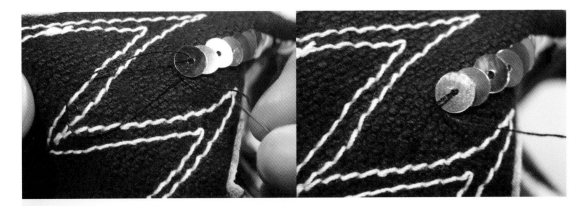

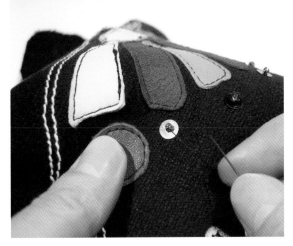

Stitch sequins onto the fabric using the following method: bring your threaded needle up through the material and centre of the sequin , then loop it as though you were making a chainstitch. Take the thread back through the centre of the sequin, then bring it up at the far edge through the loop (so that you do, indeed, make a chainstitch). Pass your needle through the centre of another sequin, loop the thread and pass the needle back down the centre of this sequin, thus repeating the process. This technique can be used to form a chain of overlapping sequins. Alternatively, to form isolated 'spots', a bead can be stitched at the centre of each sequin to secure it to the fabric.

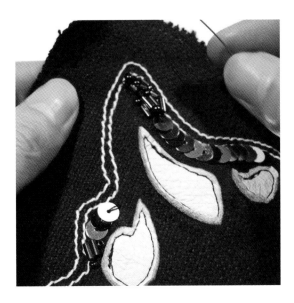

Stitch iridescent seed and bugle beads in random clusters close to and in amongst the sequins to heighten the effect of iridescence.

The finished bag front.

Punch holes for the eyelets into the bag back, using the tool that should come with your eyelet kit.

Stitch front and back together, leaving a gap for the zip.

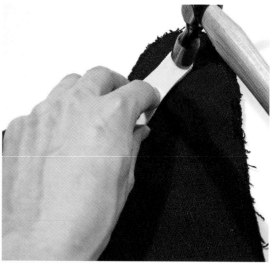

Using the existing holes as a template, punch holes in the front of the bag using the eyelet tool.

Tack the zip on, leaving it open.

Turn the bag inside out, shaping the corners with the blunt end of a pencil.

Topstitch the zip closely around its edge to hold it in position.

Cut away the excess length of zip.

Fix the eyelets into their holes.

Draw the length of furnishing cord through the eyelet holes. Tie the cord around itself in half-hitches for a decorative finish.

Tuck the free cord ends under a knot and handstitch them in position to secure.

The finished bag.

13 pattern making

Bags and purses offer a number of challenges to the maker. The design must be not just visually attractive but serve as a container or receptacle for a number of diverse items, which, depending on the occasion the bag is used for, may be of highly specific dimensions. For example, the designs in this book range from the simple Pendant Coin Purse, intended to be worn around the neck, to the City Bag, which shows a higher level of shaping within its design and incorporates a range of pockets that on the one hand may be suitable for a mobile phone, on the other, for a pair of shoes. Measurement is thus important in designing the bag pattern.

All the bags in this book 'work'; that is to say, they perform their intended function and have been designed with that function in mind. Whether the bag or purse is intended for everyday or evening purposes, the design and decoration should ideally reflect that; although highly decorative, as opposed to functional bags, can work just as well in an everyday setting.

Within this book you should have found a variety of good basic bag shapes and patterns, along with suggestions for considered fabric choices (fur fabrics, leather, denims and canvas); demonstrations as to how the bag shape can easily be manipulated using darts, tucks and gathers to create fullness; ideas for working with decorative trims and notions (eyelets, buckles, zips, rhinestones, beads,

sequins, trims, tassels, fasteners); techniques such as machined patchwork and appliqué; and methods of closure.

Most bag patterns start with a rectangle, or circle, as their basis. In fact so many bag patterns are based around rectangles that they can appear rather tedious! However, this can be circumvented by refining the shape of the pattern so it looks less obviously rectangular. For example, the handles of the Yummy Mummy bag are projected up from the main rectangular shape, which has a

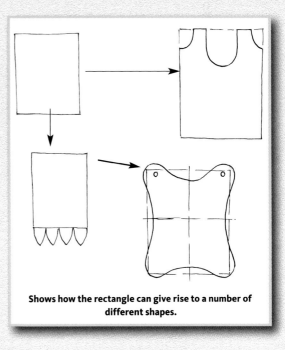

Shows how the rectangle can give rise to a number of different shapes.

semicircle cut out of the top of it. The Indian Bag's rectangular shape is disguised by tabs attached to the lower edge. The Butterfly Bag has an undulating perimeter based around a square shape.

Circles or semicircles are a good choice for basic purse patterns because they are easily gripped; the circle is a 'friendly' shape. The 'pod' shape of a number of currently fashionable bags is loosely based on a circle.

Lastly, shapes which do not fit into those two categories also fulfil a number of uses. For example, the shape of the Patchwork Mini-Rucksack is based loosely on a wedge with two right-angled triangles at either side.

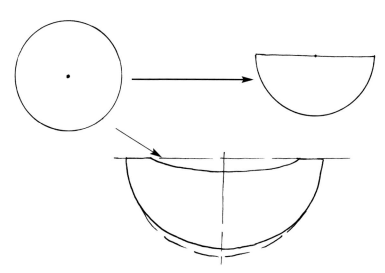

How a circle can give rise to different shapes.

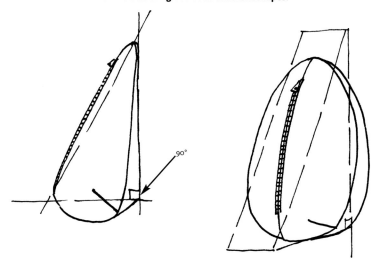

The Patchwork Tote, based on a wedge shape.

making and working with bag patterns

YOU WILL NEED

- Propelling pencil
- Drafting or putty eraser
- Fineliner pen
- Ruler (marked in both inches and centimetres if possible)
- Set square
- Protractor
- Compasses
- French curves
- Flexible curve
- Layout paper (semi-transparent, good for pattern drafting)
- Thin card (optional, for making master patterns)
- Paper scissors
- Sellotape®

As was mentioned in the preceding section, most bags begin as a rectangle. However, this can be made more exciting by manipulating the pattern. Do the following exercise: cut a rectangle from a piece of layout paper. This rectangle can now be manipulated in any way you want. It can be subdivided into several different shapes, to make pat-

tern pieces with style lines. Draw the shapes onto the rectangle, then cut them out. Tape them onto another piece of layout paper, then add seam allowance around all sides. You can now cut each piece from the same or different fabrics. Experimenting with sewing together different combinations will give different effects.

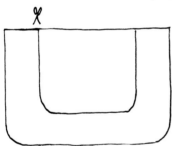

Cutting into a rectangular shape.

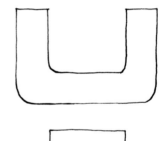

Shapes formed from the original rectangular shape.

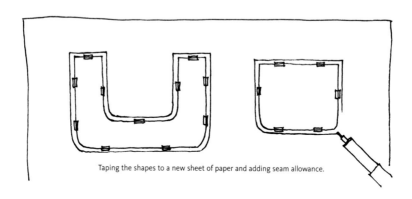

Taping the shapes to a new sheet of paper and adding seam allowance.

When creating an alternative outline shape, consider the number of sides you want to be symmetrical. Will both sides be mirror-images of each other, or will the bag have four-fold symmetry? Depending on which you choose, it will be necessary to draw one part of the pattern and then fold it along the relevant axis once or twice; since the layout paper is semi-transparent, the pattern can be traced using the original lines. Two-fold symmetry is generally the most pleasing.

You can gather, dart or tuck one or both edges to create fullness in the shape. This will, however, have the effect of reducing the length along the gathered, darted or tucked side. If you intend to keep certain dimensions, you will need to allow for this in the pattern.

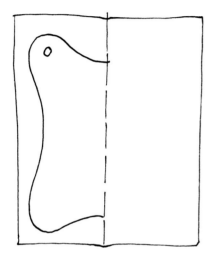 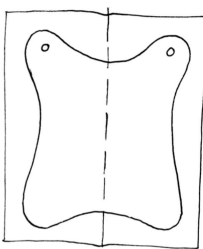

Symmetrical objects with 2-fold symmetry:
drawing one half of the design on one half of the page, then tracing the mirror image onto the opposite half.

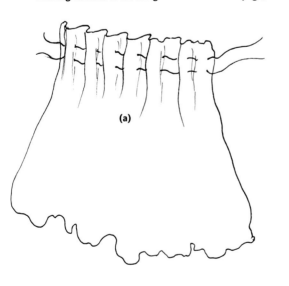 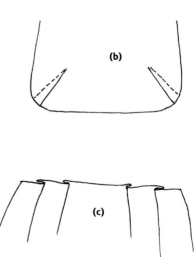

a) Gathers, b) darts, c) tucks.

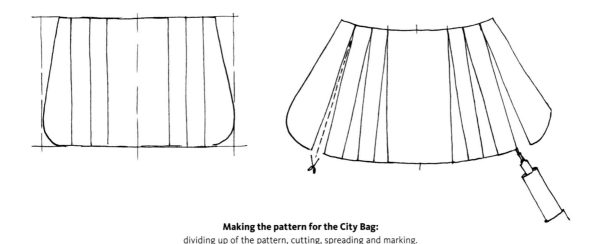

Making the pattern for the City Bag:
dividing up of the pattern, cutting, spreading and marking.

In order to conserve dimensions, especially when adding tucks, or to add extra fullness to part of a bag, the cut-and-spread method of pattern cutting can be used. To demonstrate how this works it may be useful (especially for beginners) to try the following exercise:

Divide your basic bag shape into 2.5 cm (1 in.) sections, at the points you want it to show flare. Cut down the lines dividing these sections, using paper scissors, working from one side to the other. Do not cut all the way to the other side. Leave a small 'hinge' joining each section; you will find that there is movement and flexibility at these points.

Then, place the shape carefully on a fresh sheet of paper. Working one section at a time, use Sellotape® to tape down each section onto this sheet of paper. You will observe that the sections can be moved independently of each other. Tape the sections down so that there is about 2.5 cm (1 in.) between the corners of adjacent sections, on the free sides.

Taping down the sections gives you the basis for your pattern shape. In order to refine the shape of the pattern, it will be necessary to draw around the sections using a smooth curve and your propelling pencil and other drawing materials such as French curves and flexible curves. These give a more pleasing finish than drawing entirely freehand. Again, for symmetrical items, remember to fold and draw in the outline shapes along axes of symmetry. Drawing over your lines with a fineliner will also define the shape more

clearly. This type of cutting, called 'cut and spread', will ensure that one side of the item retains its original length; this will, however, have the effect of increasing the opposite side in length. The distances between sections may be increased or decreased according to the amount of fullness desired.

Cut the shape out with paper scissors and place it on another sheet of paper. Draw round the shape; once removed, the shape of the pattern should again be checked and any aberrations in the pattern line redrawn correctly. Cut the pattern out using paper scissors. You may want to further refine the shape at this stage, or, in the event of your being entirely satisfied with your shape, the pattern should now be ready to make up by sticking together in 'rough' format.

Cut sufficient pattern pieces with which to make the bag from. A lot of bags simply have a front and back, but gusseted bags will have one or more side gussets. It will be necessary to measure around the edges of the bag side in order to get an idea of the length of the side pieces, which are usually in the form of a rectangular strip. Especially if the corners are curved, extra ease may also need to be allowed.

When you have cut out all the pattern pieces, stick them together using Sellotape® along all the edges that require seaming. The information gained at this stage is invaluable as it gives a good idea of the dimensions of your bag and the types of object that can be carried. There may also be visual elements of the design that need to be adjusted.

Make a note of the design adjustments that need to be made; if necessary, draw them on the 3-D shape using a fineliner. Then remove the Sellotape® or cut down the joins between the paper shapes carefully. Redraw the pattern if necessary.

When you are happy with the pattern, tape it to another piece of paper, and mark the edges. Decide on a seam allowance – I would advocate 0.6 cm($^1/_4$ in.) for smaller bags in thinner fabric, 1 cm ($^3/_8$ in.) for large bags using thicker fabric. Measure it from the relevant edge, and mark it in.

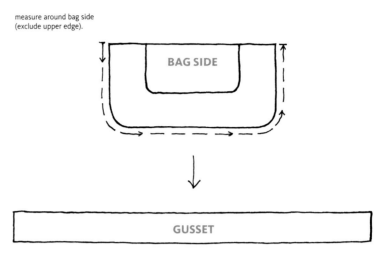

measure around bag side (exclude upper edge).

BAG SIDE

GUSSET

Making a gusset with knowledge of the bag side measurements.

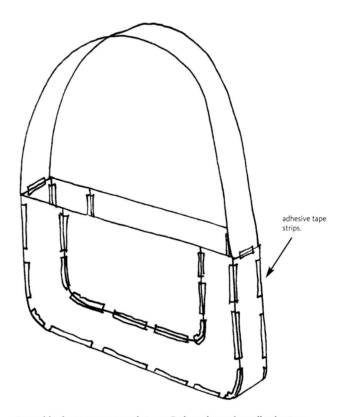

adhesive tape strips.

Assemble the paper pattern into a 3-D shape bag using adhesive tape.

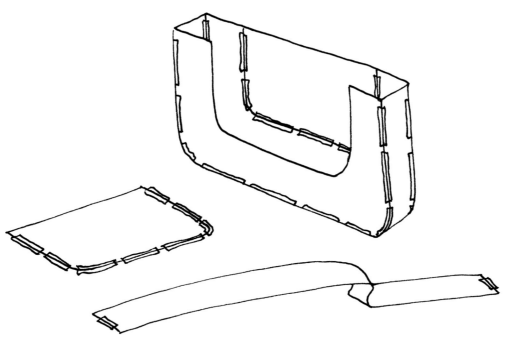

Disassembly of the 3-D paper shape in readiness for making a master pattern.

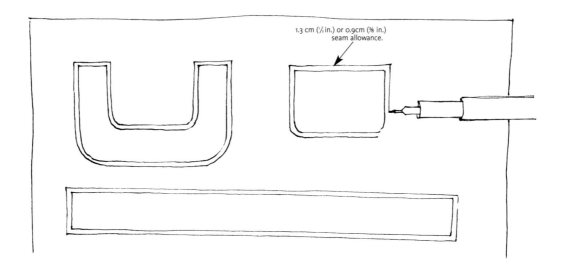

1.3 cm (½ in.) or 0.9cm (⅜ in.) seam allowance.

Placing patterns on a new sheet of paper, marking seam allowance.

Remove the pattern. Take your preliminary pattern and check it against the final pattern to ensure that there are no deviations.

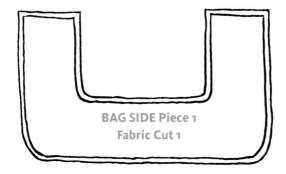

BAG SIDE Piece 1
Fabric Cut 1

Pattern marked with information.

The pattern can then be marked according to its design position, type of fabric to be used (for example, fabric, wadding or lining) and number of pieces needed.

You may want to make a master pattern from thin card if you are particularly satisfied with it and want to use it over a long period of time. I personally prefer thin paper patterns as they allow for better readjustment.

Pockets should be designed with their function in mind, the objects that they are designed to carry measured, and a paper pattern made beforehand to check fit. The mobile phone pockets in this book should carry most standard size mobile phones. (However, they are not designed to carry Blackberries!)

So that the mobile phone will not 'pop out' of its pocket easily, draw the pocket pattern to a slightly larger size than the phone and then fold the excess fabric to the corners to shape the pocket.

For facings I normally allow at least 5 cm (2 in.) from the relevant edges, although this will depend on your bag design and placement of all the other design elements such as pockets and handles. I would recommend a facing or self-fabric lining where extra strength needs to be added to the bag, particularly in the closure or handle area; it may also look neater than the edge of a lining fabric placed at the edge of a bag. Facing patterns need to be considered in conjunction with lining patterns and constructed

accordingly, with seam allowances added all round and the correct amount of fabric subtracted.

Within the book you may observe that I present separate lining patterns for some items and not for others. Where separate lining patterns are present this is usually to make your life easier where I have also added facings. It also serves to demonstrate the amount that needs to be subtracted to create a 'comfortable' lining that does not affect the shape of the bag and lead to an 'overstuffed', unsightly appearance when the bag is turned right side out. Where gathers are present the question of lining affecting the shape of the outer will not matter so much, as the gathers will hide the shape of the lining much more easily than in a bag with a very precise shape. Where a binding trim is used, the lining and outer fabrics will in any case be joined flush, with the binding covering both edges.

With fusible fabrics, I often use the same pattern as I would for the outer fabric and then trim a constant 0.6 cm ($^1/_4$ in.) all the way round, which saves having to make an extra pattern for the fusible and removes extra bulk from the seams, whilst still strengthening the bag.

design drawings and inspiration

Professional designers in industry usually create design drawings and specifications sheets with attached fabric swatches. Spec sheets are detailed annotated drawings which indicate the finished item's dimensions in numerical terms, and any construction details, such as single or double seams. It is usual, when making items on an industrial scale, to provide the manufacturer with this type of drawing.

Design drawings are the 'fashion' illustrations the general public knows and loves. These show the item in a more artistic context, without the specifications that are typical of the spec. sheet. Design drawings vary in quality, from the highly finished to the sketchy; 'quality' in this case can also be defined as descriptive of a particular designer's drawing style. It is important to have, or source, drawing skills that illustrate your work well to others (including customers), and it is seen as good practice to be able to present them professionally in a folio or presentation case. Practice putting your ideas onto paper whenever you can; fine-liners or disposable technical drawing pens give a crisp and professional feel and are handy

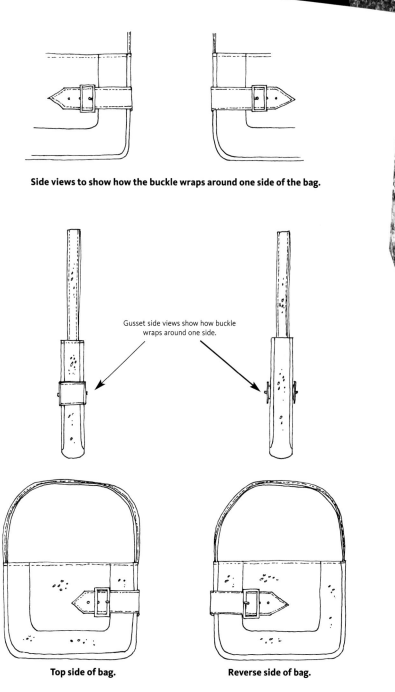

Side views to show how the buckle wraps around one side of the bag.

Gusset side views show how buckle wraps around one side.

Top side of bag.

Reverse side of bag.

for beginners; work done in them tends to 'look good', irrespective of the artist's skills! Try, if you can, to convey the shape and hang of the item, as well as the material in which it is constructed.

There are a number of books on design development, which reduces the necessity for coverage in this book. Inspirations vary enormously, whether they are from a materials or practically-oriented standpoint or an 'ideas'-based one. In practice most work is often a mixture of the two, where aesthetic insight is successfully used to present materials to their best advantage. Personally I would advise that beginners start by getting a feel for materials and construction before moving on to more 'ideas'-based projects. This will be extremely helpful as it gives one a solid base from which to eventually develop a personal style and way of working with materials. I would initially recommend perusing fashion magazines and shops for inspiration, construction techniques and fashionable shapes, combining ideas and creating an item from these inspirations. This also enables one to obtain a sound knowledge of prevailing fashions and basic shapes that can be restyled or decorated.

Fashion drawing of a bag made in leatherette, conveying style, material type and approximate scale.
The drawing was made from a photograph using a propelling pencil. The bag was coloured using markers, then worked over again in pencil to emphasise folds and textures. Note how judicious use of media conveys the surface texture and semi-shiny qualities of leather and letherette. Note also how the style line between different coloured materials acts as a design element.

patterns

Canvas Bag

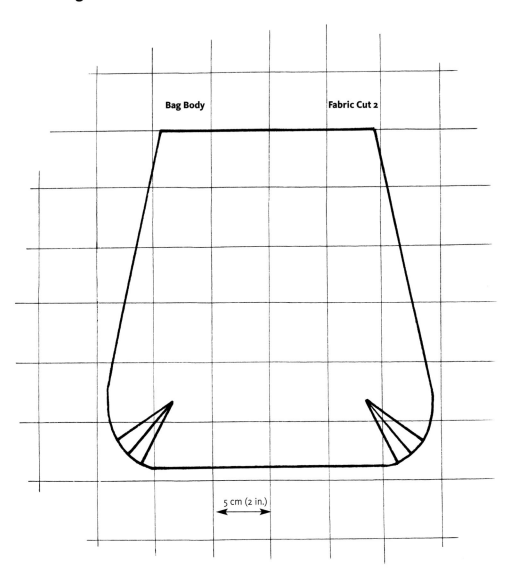

Bag Body

Fabric Cut 2

5 cm (2 in.)

Yummy Mummy Bag (1)

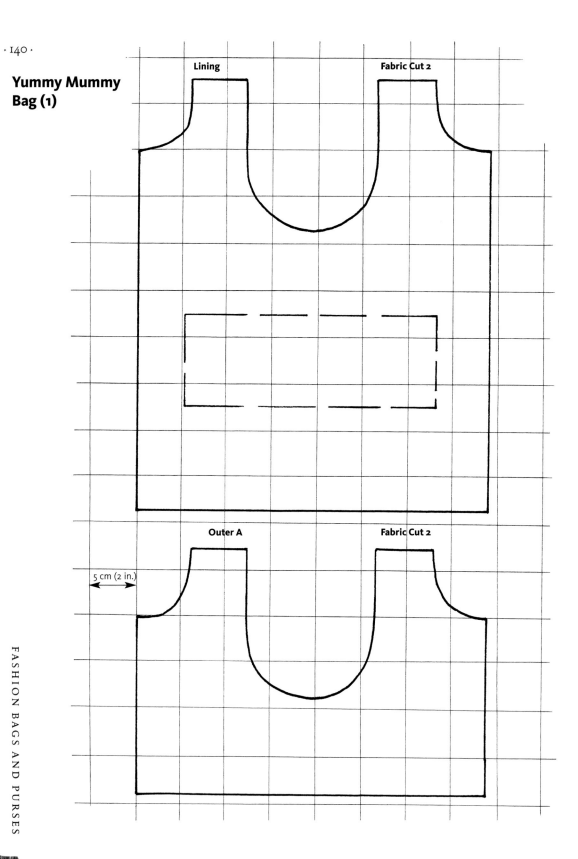

Lining

Fabric Cut 2

Outer A

Fabric Cut 2

5 cm (2 in.)

Yummy Mummy Bag (2)

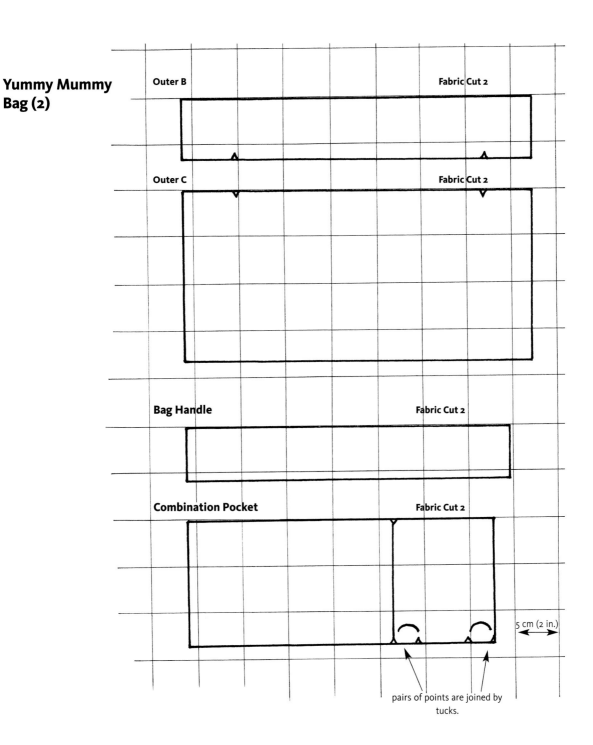

Outer B   Fabric Cut 2

Outer C   Fabric Cut 2

Bag Handle   Fabric Cut 2

Combination Pocket   Fabric Cut 2

5 cm (2 in.)

pairs of points are joined by tucks.

Yummy Mummy
Bag (3)

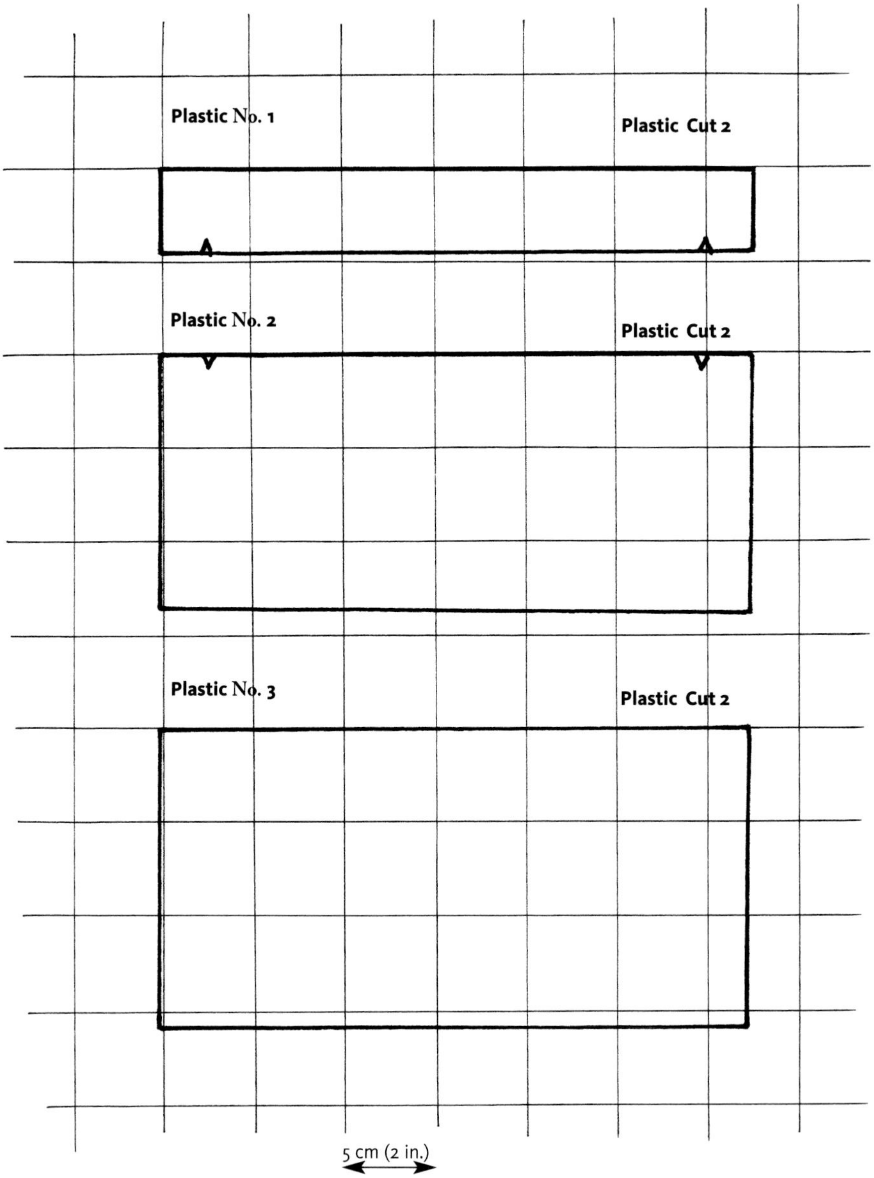

Plastic No. 1

Plastic Cut 2

Plastic No. 2

Plastic Cut 2

Plastic No. 3

Plastic Cut 2

5 cm (2 in.)

Pendant Purse

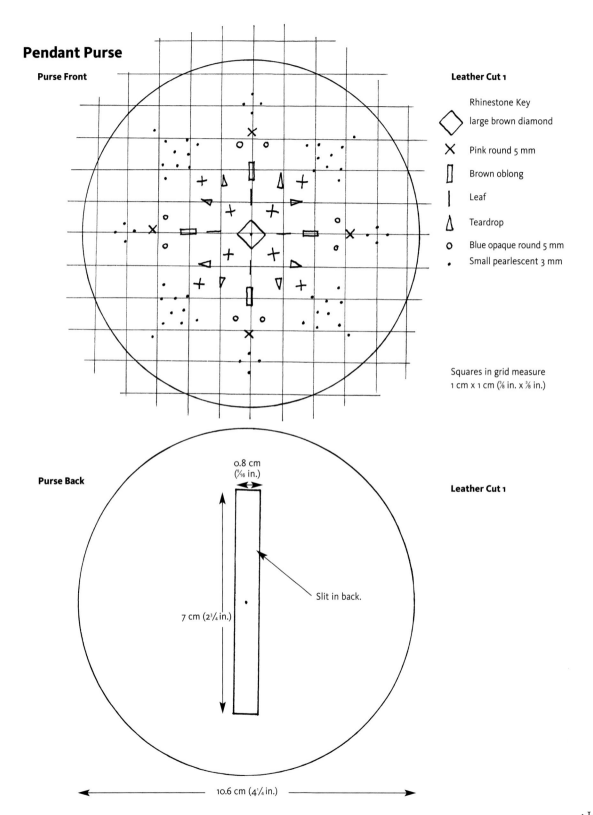

Purse Front

Leather Cut 1

Rhinestone Key

◇ large brown diamond

✕ Pink round 5 mm

▯ Brown oblong

| Leaf

△ Teardrop

○ Blue opaque round 5 mm

• Small pearlescent 3 mm

Squares in grid measure
1 cm x 1 cm (⅜ in. x ⅜ in.)

Purse Back

Leather Cut 1

0.8 cm
(⁵⁄₁₆ in.)

Slit in back.

7 cm (2¾ in.)

10.6 cm (4¼ in.)

Exotic Fabrics Bag

Lining   **Lining Cut 2**

Quilted Side A   **Fabric Cut 2**
Wadding Cut 1

Position for handle.

Quilted Side B   **Fabric Cut 2**
Wadding Cut 1

Position for handle.

Notch marks point at which piece joins bag side.

5 cm (2 in.)

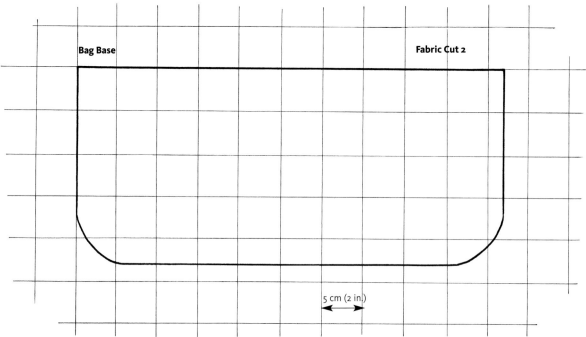

Bag Base   **Fabric Cut 2**

5 cm (2 in.)

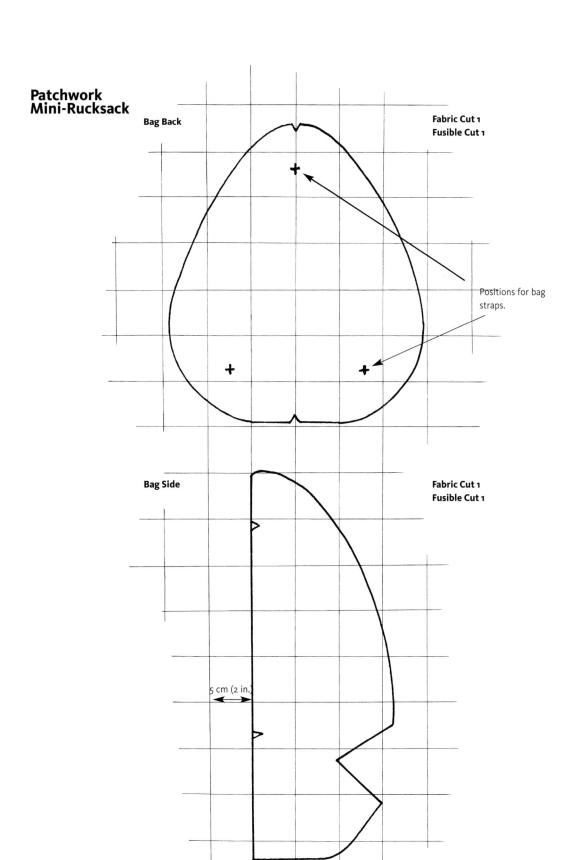

Patchwork
Mini-Rucksack

Bag Back

Fabric Cut 1
Fusible Cut 1

Positions for bag straps.

Bag Side

Fabric Cut 1
Fusible Cut 1

5 cm (2 in.)

Faux Fur Shoulder Bag

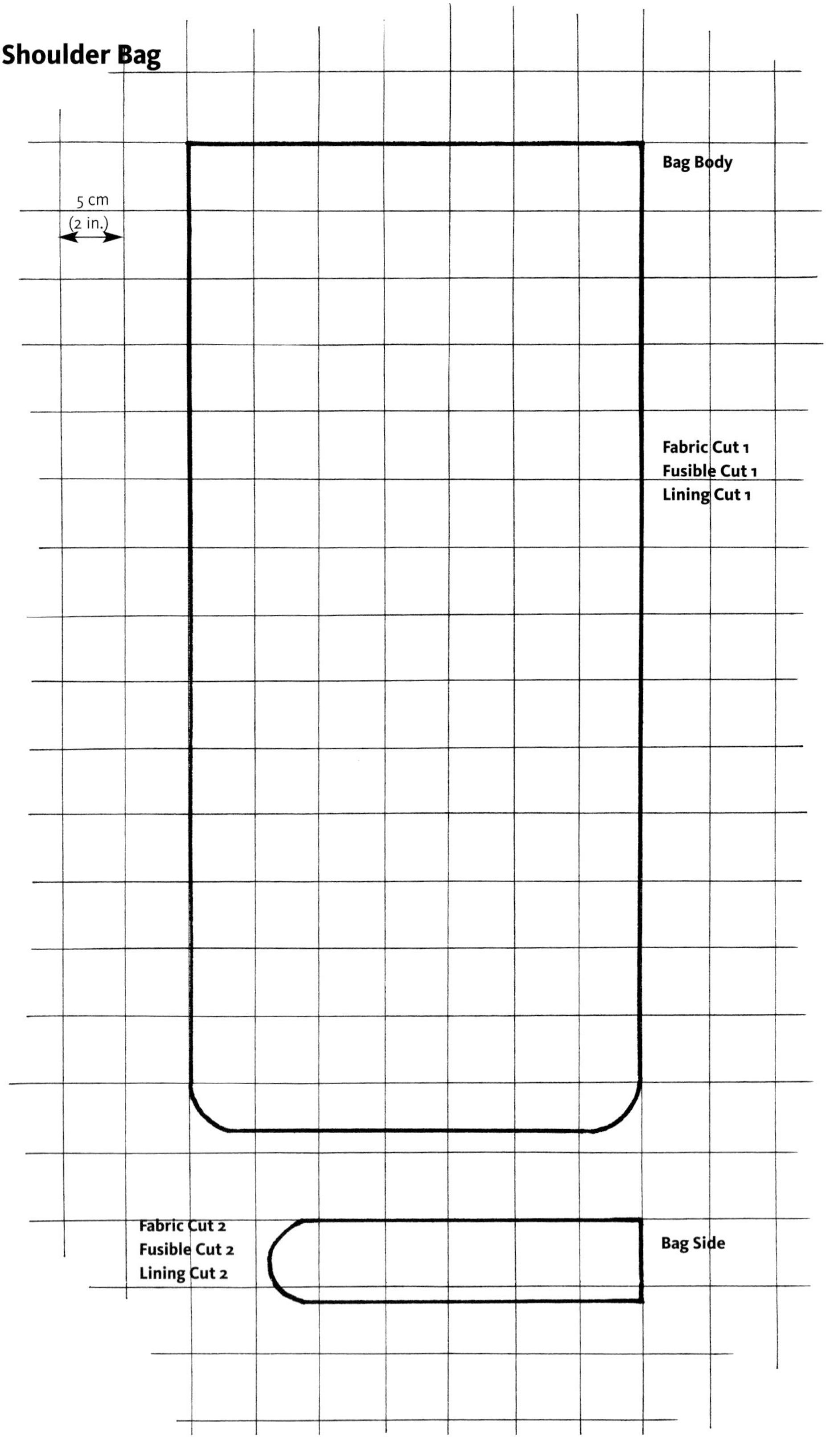

5 cm
(2 in.)

Bag Body

Fabric Cut 1
Fusible Cut 1
Lining Cut 1

Fabric Cut 2
Fusible Cut 2
Lining Cut 2

Bag Side

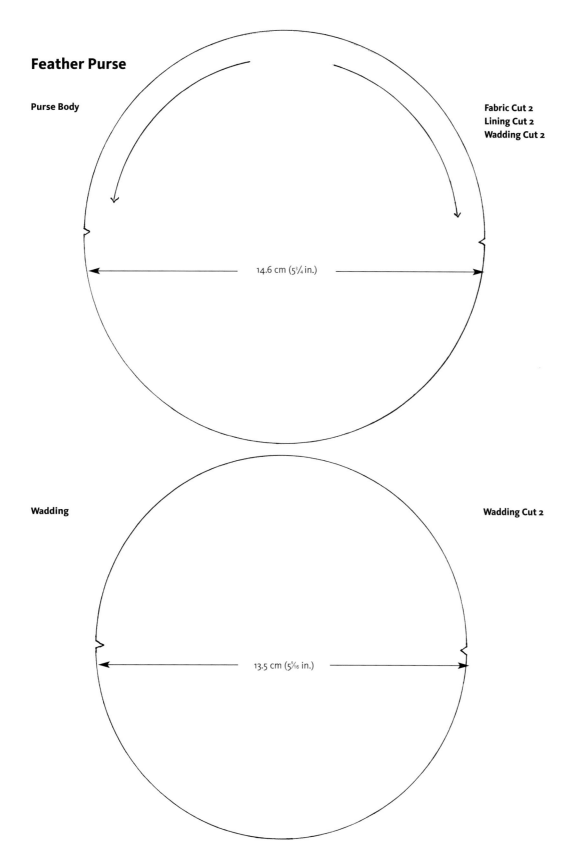

Feather Purse

Purse Body

Fabric Cut 2
Lining Cut 2
Wadding Cut 2

14.6 cm (5¾ in.)

Wadding

Wadding Cut 2

13.5 cm (5⁵⁄₁₆ in.)

Indian Bag

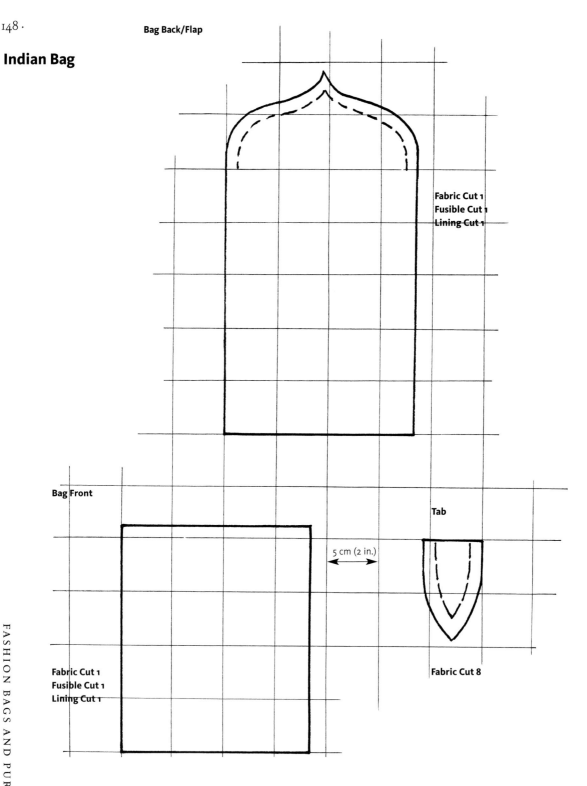

Bag Back/Flap

Fabric Cut 1
Fusible Cut 1
Lining Cut 1

Bag Front

Fabric Cut 1
Fusible Cut 1
Lining Cut 1

5 cm (2 in.)

Tab

Fabric Cut 8

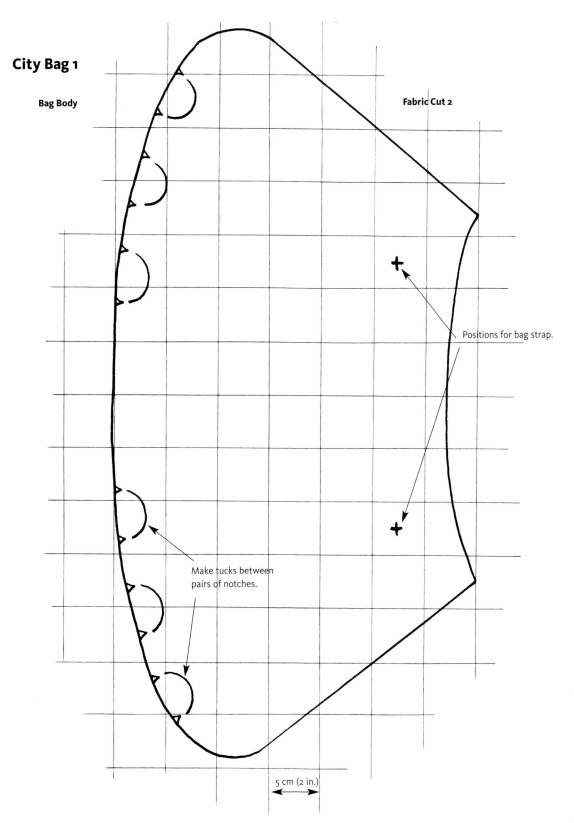

City Bag 1

Bag Body

Fabric Cut 2

Positions for bag strap.

Make tucks between pairs of notches.

5 cm (2 in.)

City Bag 2

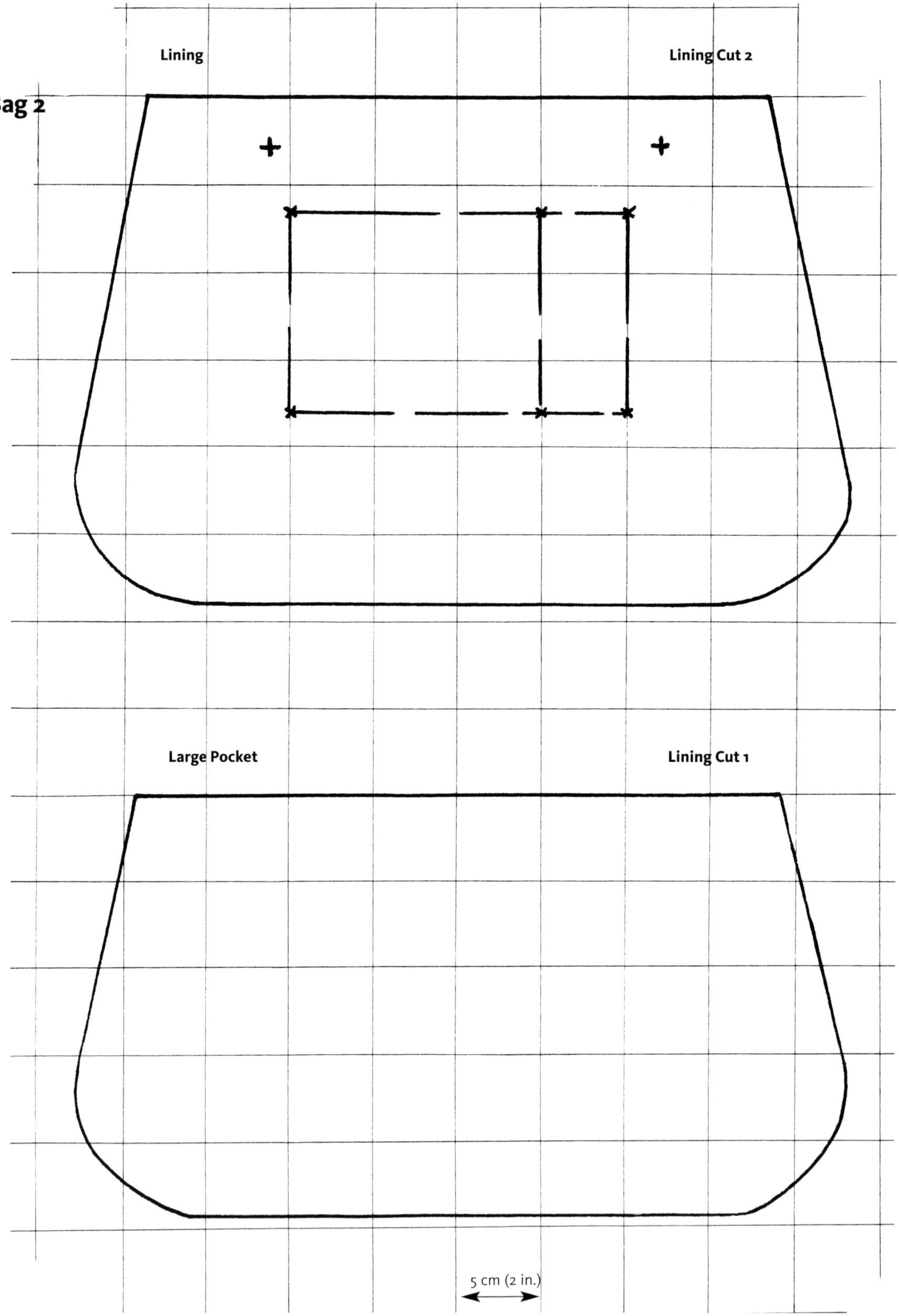

Lining

Lining Cut 2

Large Pocket

Lining Cut 1

5 cm (2 in.)

City Bag 3

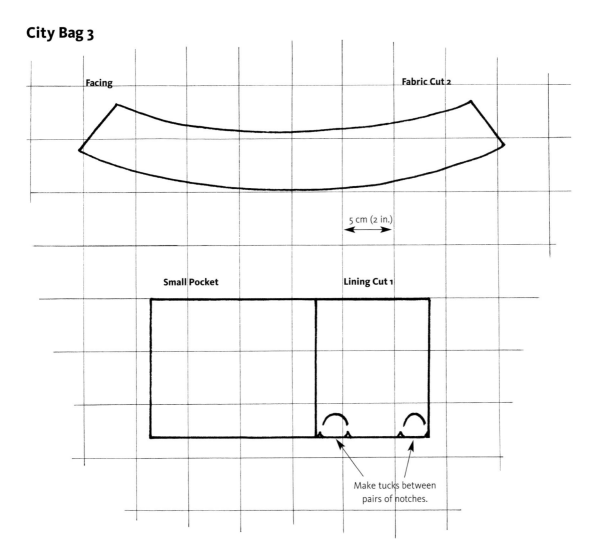

Facing

Fabric Cut 2

5 cm (2 in.)

Small Pocket

Lining Cut 1

Make tucks between
pairs of notches.

Butterfly Bag (Upper left)

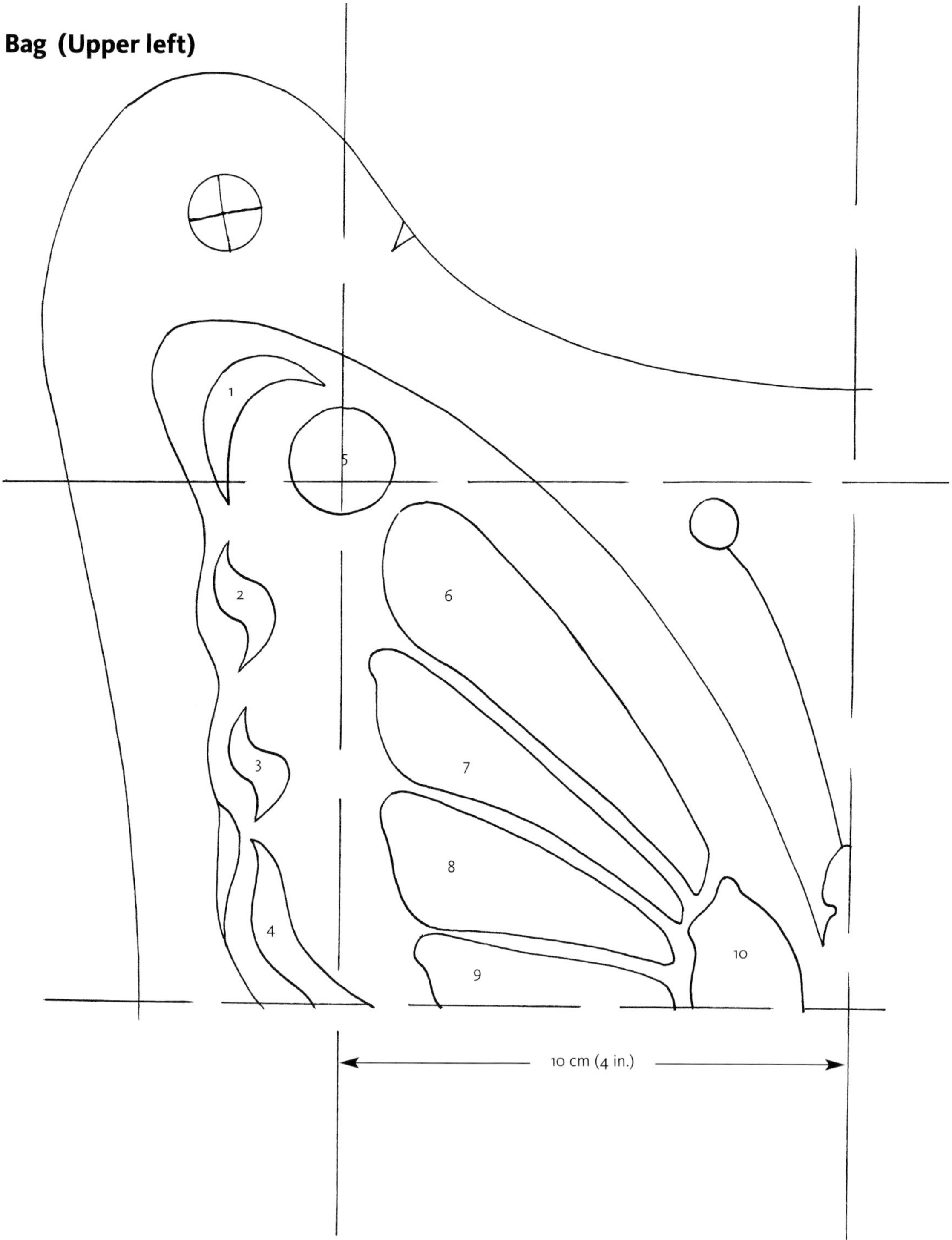

1

5

2

6

3

7

8

4

10

9

10 cm (4 in.)

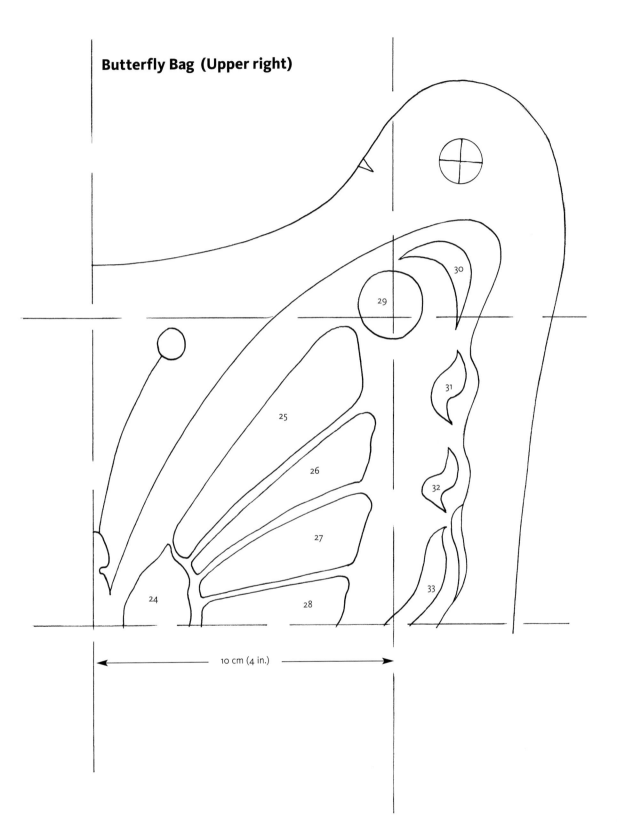

Butterfly Bag (Upper right)

24
25
26
27
28
29
30
31
32
33

10 cm (4 in.)

Butterfly Bag (Lower left)

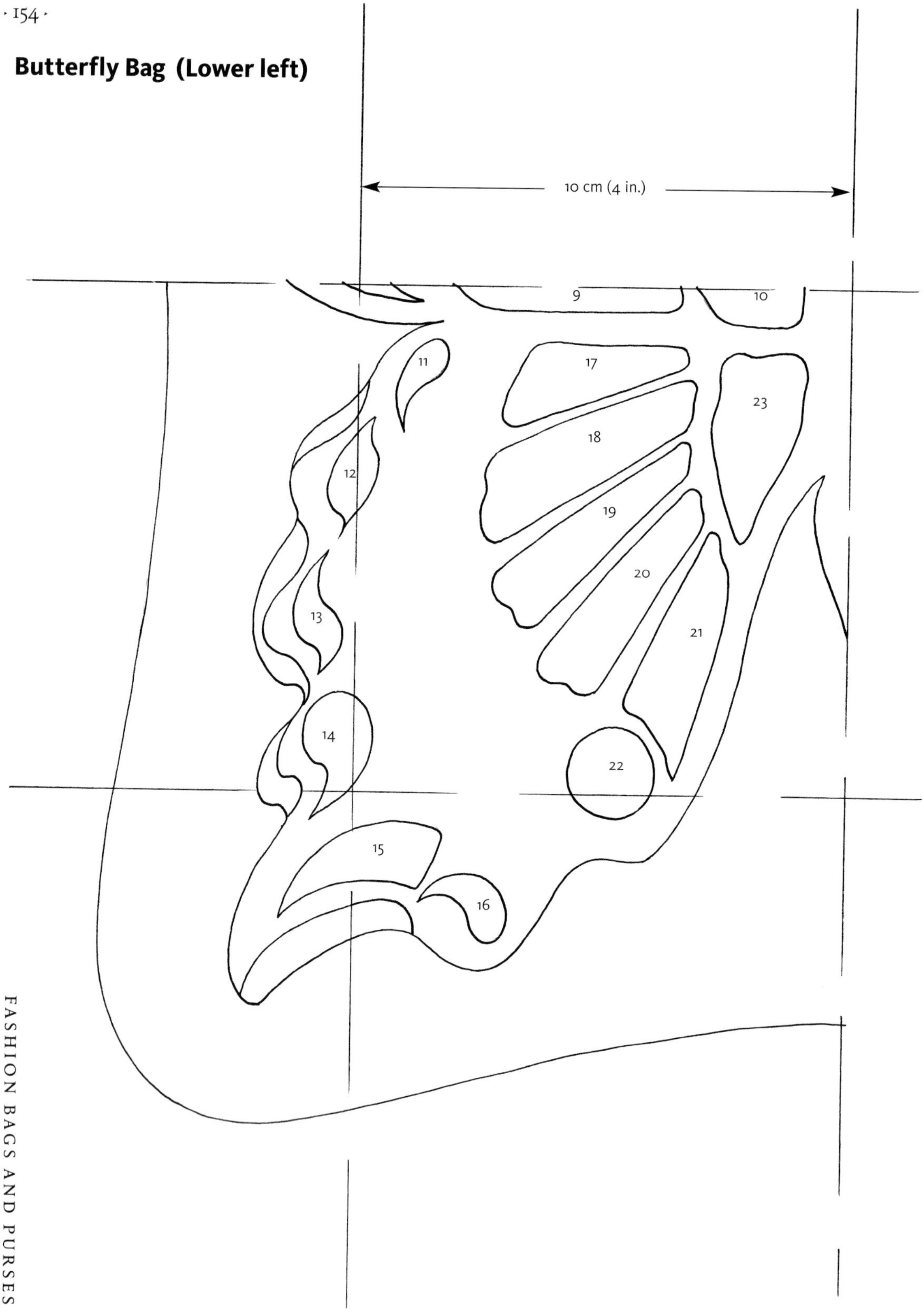

10 cm (4 in.)

9

10

11

17

23

12

18

19

13

20

14

21

22

15

16

Butterfly Bag (Lower right)

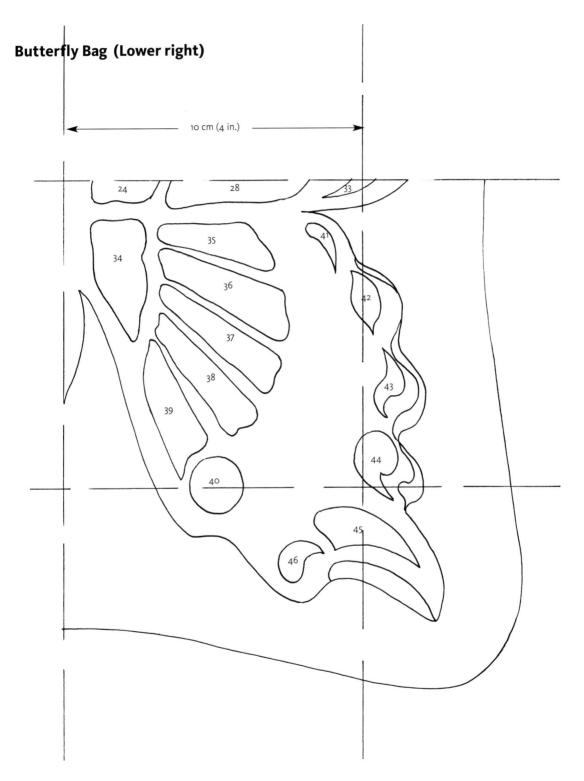

10 cm (4 in.)

24   28   33

34   35

36

37

38

39

40

41

42

43

44

45

46

glossary

Many of the terms are already covered in Chapter 2; however, here is a list of items that may be unfamiliar or are specific to bagmaking and pattern construction.

Buckram, millinery – tough openweave fabric impregnated with glue, used in millinery hat bases; may also on occasion be used for bag bottoms. The term is a generic one and may also be applied to other types of stiffener such as the buckram used in collars.

Circle template – a piece of drawing equipment with circles of varying sizes, useful for positioning buckle holes and drawing curved corners in pattern drafting.

Copydex® – a type of non-toxic rubber cement suitable for use in bag construction.

Drill, fusible – a canvas backed with heat fixable glue that can be used to provide stability for medium-weight bag fabrics.

French curves – drawing implements with a variety of shaped curves in varying sizes, that are useful for pattern drafting.

Fusibles – fabrics coated with glue on one or both sides that give stability to outer fabrics and are fixed by ironing.

Layout paper – thin semi-transparent paper useful for sketching, pattern-making and drafting.

Polypropylene webbing – a tough woven polypropylene braid suitable for bag carrying straps.

Purse frame – a frame into which the fabric body of a purse is fixed, also comprising a clip closure.

RS – right side.

RSS – right sides.

Style line – a line along which the pattern is cut, which also has a decorative function.

Vilene® – trade name for a variety of fusibles of different types, defined by number.

WS – wrong side.

WSS – wrong sides.

bibliography

This is a brief list of books that may be interesting from the point of view of pattern-cutting, construction or design:

Aldrich, Winifred, *Fabric, Form and Flat Pattern Cutting*, pub. Blackwell Science Ltd., 1996, ISBN 0-632-03917-5.
(pattern-cutting)

Beverly, Deena, *Brilliant Bags*, pub. Mitchell Beazley 2006, ISBN-13: 978- 1 8453 3178 8, ISBN-10: 1-8453-3178-8
(construction, design, inspiration, styling)

Evans, Deborah (ed.), *The Hamlyn Complete Sewing Course,* pub. Hamlyn Publishing Group Ltd., 1989, ISBN 0-600-564495-9.
(sewing, construction)

Johnson, Anna, *Handbags: The Power of the Purse*, pub. Workman Publishing Company, Inc., 2002, ISBN 0-7611-2377-6.
(history)

stockists

Most of the suppliers of fabric used in this book are located within London's West End (nearest tubes: Oxford St, Tottenham Court Rd., Bond St, Piccadilly Circus) and are within easy walking distance of each other. Where possible websites and email addresses have also been provided.

Barnett Lawson Trimmings, 16–17 Little Portland St, London W1W 8NE (wholesalers): lurex tassels for Indian Bag, Chapter 10.
Tel: 020 7636 8591 Email: info@bltrimmings.com
www.bltrimmings.com

Berwick St. Cloth Shop, 14 Berwick St, London W1F 0PP: fake fur fabric, Faux Fur Shoulder Bag, Chapter 8.
Tel: 020 7287 2881 Email: berwickstcloth@aol.com
www.thesilksociety.com

Borovick Fabrics Ltd., 16 Berwick St, London W1F 0HP: leather pieces for Canvas Bag, Chapter 3; leather for Pendant Purse, Chapter 5; navy denim for City Bag, Chapter 11; leather pieces for Butterfly Bag, Chapter 12.
Tel: 020 7437 2180 Email: borovickfabrics@btclick.com
www.borovickfabricsltd.co.uk.

Broadwick Silks, 9–11 Broadwick St, London W1F 0DB: silk for Feather Purse, Chapter 9. Tel: 020 7734 3320
Email: broadwicksilks@aol.com www.thesilksociety.com

Cloth House, 47 Berwick St, London W1F 8SJ, also 98 Berwick St, London W1F 0QJ: Op Art fabric and plastic lining for Yummy Mummy Bag, Chapter 4; canvas for Canvas Bag, Chapter 3; lamé fabric for Exotic Fabrics bag, Chapter 6; tie silks for Patchwork Mini-Rucksack, Chapter 7; Indian fabrics and trims for Indian Bag, Chapter 10; mesh fabric for City Bag, Chapter 11; canvas for Butterfly Bag, Chapter 12.
Tel: 020 7485 6247 Email: info@clothhouse.com

Creative Beadcraft, 20 Beak St, London W1F 9RE: rhinestones and thong for Pendant Purse, Chapter 5; large sew-on rhinestones and seed beads for Feather Purse, Chapter 9; bells for Indian Bag, Chapter 10; beads for Butterfly Bag, Chapter 12.
Tel: 020 7629 9964 Email: tracey@creativebeadcraft.co.uk
www.creative-beadcraft.co.uk.

Kleins, 5 Noel St, London W1F 8GD: rings for bag handle supports, Exotic Fabrics Bag, Chapter 6; buckles and yellow polypropylene webbing for Patchwork Mini-Rucksack, Chapter 7; purse frame for Feather Purse, Chapter 9; sequins for Butterfly Bag, Chapter 12
Tel: 020 7437 6162 www.kleins.co.uk.

MacCulloch & Wallis, 25–26 Dering St, London W1S 1AT: buckles, silk satin ribbon binding and snap fastener for Canvas Bag, Chapter 3; silk satin ribbon binding for Pendant Purse, Chapter 5; ribbon for bag handles, Exotic Fabrics Bag, Chapter 6; red binding, black Velcro and black polypropylene webbing for Faux Fur Shoulder Bag, Chapter 8; feather trims for Feather Purse, Chapter 9; large buttons for City Bag, Chapter 11; suede ribbon, cord and eyelets for Butterfly Bag, Chapter 12, all buckles and all satin and poplin linings; all zips; all fusibles including wadding.
Tel: 020 7629 0311 Email: macculloch@psilink.co.uk
www.macculloch-wallis.co.uk

Skin Machine, 25 Kensington Church St, London W8 4LL: leather (from discounted leather skirts) for Butterfly Bag, Chapter 12. Tel: 020 7937 3297

index